# WHY NAGASAKI?

## UNDERSTANDING THE WHY AND HOW OF THE SECOND ATOMIC STRIKE

TARUN MAJUMDER

Made with ♥ on the Notion Press Platform
www.notionpress.com

# Contents

# Contents

# Foreword

Introduction to "Why Nagasaki?"

On the morning of August 9, 1945, the serene city of Nagasaki was engulfed in an inferno of unimaginable power. The second atomic bomb ever used in warfare, codenamed "Fat Man," was dropped, resulting in massive destruction and loss of life. This moment, just three days after the bombing of Hiroshima, not only marked the climax of World War II but also etched Nagasaki into the annals of history. This book, "Why Nagasaki?", seeks to unravel the complex web of decisions, strategies, and circumstances that led to the bombing of Nagasaki. It explores four pivotal questions: Why was the bombing necessary at all? Why was there a second bombing only three days after Hiroshima? Why was Nagasaki chosen as the target? And what were the technological differences and scientific motivations behind the bombings?

Why Was Bombing Necessary?

To understand the necessity of the atomic bombings, we must first delve into the context of World War II's final stages. By mid-1945, the war in Europe had ended, but the Pacific War raged on with brutal intensity. The United States, along with its Allies, faced a formidable Japanese military that showed no signs of surrender. The Japanese defence strategy was one of total war, with military leaders willing to sacrifice countless lives in a bid to defend their homeland.

President Harry S. Truman, newly in office after Franklin D. Roosevelt's death, faced an agonizing decision. An invasion of Japan was projected to result in astronomical Allied casualties, with estimates ranging from hundreds of thousands to potentially over a million. Japanese civilian casualties would also be enormous, given the expected resistance. The firebombing of Japanese cities had already caused immense destruction and loss of life, yet Japan remained defiant.

In July 1945, the Potsdam Conference brought together Truman, British Prime Minister Winston Churchill (later replaced by Clement Attlee), and Soviet Premier Joseph Stalin. During this conference, Truman received word of the successful Trinity test—the first detonation of a nuclear weapon. Armed with this new weapon, Truman and his advisors saw an opportunity to end the war swiftly and decisively without the need for a costly invasion.

The Potsdam Declaration issued on July 26, 1945, called for Japan's unconditional surrender, warning of "prompt and utter destruction" if they refused. The declaration did not mention the atomic bomb explicitly, but it made clear the dire consequences of continued resistance. When Japan failed to respond adequately, Truman made the decision to deploy the atomic bomb to force a swift end to the war.

Why a Second Bombing Only Three Days After Hiroshima?

The decision to drop a second bomb so soon after Hiroshima is deeply intertwined with the strategic and psychological objectives of the United States. The bombing of Hiroshima on August 6, 1945, caused unprecedented destruction, killing tens of thousands instantly and levelling the city. However, Japan did not immediately surrender. The Japanese government, particularly its military factions, remained divided on the response to the Potsdam Declaration and the Hiroshima bombing.

Truman and his advisers believed that demonstrating the capability and willingness to use multiple atomic bombs was crucial. They wanted to convey to Japan—and to the world—that the United States possessed a powerful new weapon and was prepared to use it until Japan surrendered unconditionally. The rapid succession of the bombings was intended to shock the Japanese leadership into realizing that further resistance was futile and that more bombings could follow if they did not surrender.

Moreover, there was a concern that delaying the second bombing would give Japan time to regroup, possibly relocate important facilities, or develop strategies to mitigate the impact of future bombings. By acting swiftly, the United States aimed to maintain the element of surprise and overwhelming force.

Why Was Nagasaki Selected?

Nagasaki was not the primary target for the second bombing; the original target was the city of Kokura. On the morning of August 9, the B-29 bomber Bockscar, piloted by Major Charles Sweeney, was scheduled to drop the "Fat Man" bomb on Kokura. However, the city was obscured by clouds and smoke from previous bombings, making visual targeting impossible.

After three unsuccessful bombing runs over Kokura, Sweeney made the decision to proceed to the secondary target: Nagasaki. The choice of Nagasaki as a target was based on its industrial and military significance. The city was home to the Mitsubishi Shipyards, Steel and Arms Works, and other factories contributing to Japan's war effort. Its geographical location and the presence of key facilities made it a strategic target for demonstrating the devastating power of the atomic bomb.

Despite being a secondary target, Nagasaki was heavily impacted. The bomb detonated over the Urakami Valley, an area with dense industrial infrastructure and residential neighbourhoods. The hilly terrain somewhat contained the blast, but the destruction was still immense, and the loss of life was catastrophic.

Technological Differences and Scientific Motivations

The atomic bombs dropped on Hiroshima and Nagasaki were not identical; they represented different technological approaches to harnessing nuclear energy for warfare. Understanding these differences sheds light on the scientific motivations and strategic considerations behind their deployment.

The bomb dropped on Hiroshima, "Little Boy," was a uranium-based bomb that used a gun-type design. In this design, two sub-critical masses of uranium-235 were brought together by a conventional explosive charge to achieve a supercritical mass and initiate a nuclear chain reaction. This type of bomb was simpler in design and did not require extensive testing to ensure reliability.

In contrast, the bomb dropped on Nagasaki, "Fat Man," was a plutonium-based bomb that used an implosion design. Plutonium-239 has different properties compared to uranium-235, including a higher rate of spontaneous fission, which made a gun-type design impractical. Instead, the implosion design used conventional explosives arranged symmetrically around a plutonium core. When detonated, these explosives compressed the plutonium core to a supercritical state, initiating the chain reaction.

The choice to use two different types of bombs was driven by several factors. Firstly, it allowed the United States to demonstrate and test both designs under combat conditions. This provided valuable data on the effectiveness, yield, and fallout of each type of bomb. The rapid succession of the bombings also served to reinforce the perception that the United States had an arsenal of different types of nuclear weapons, adding to the psychological pressure on Japan to surrender.

Moreover, the use of two different bombs highlighted the technological advancements achieved by the Manhattan Project. The success of both designs underscored the scientific and engineering prowess of the United States, serving as a deterrent to potential adversaries in the post-war world, particularly the Soviet Union.

Scientific Tests and Immediate Investigations

The immediate aftermath of the bombings also saw a concerted effort to understand and measure the effects of the atomic explosions. Scientific teams were dispatched to both Hiroshima and Nagasaki to gather data and assess the impact of the bombs. These investigations were crucial for understanding the power of nuclear weapons and their implications for future warfare.

Within days of the bombings, teams of scientists, military personnel, and medical experts were flown to the sites. In Nagasaki, these teams included members from the Manhattan Project and other military research units. Their mission was to collect data on the blast effects, radiation levels, and medical consequences.

The scientists conducted a range of tests and measurements. They examined the radius of destruction, the types of damage caused by the blast, and the spread of radioactive fallout. They also studied the immediate health effects on the survivors, including burns, radiation sickness, and psychological trauma. This data was vital for developing a comprehensive understanding of the bomb's impact and for refining nuclear weapons technology.

The investigations were not without challenges. The devastated infrastructure and the ongoing suffering of the survivors made it difficult to conduct thorough scientific studies. Nonetheless, the data collected from these early investigations laid the groundwork for future nuclear research and informed international discussions on the control and use of nuclear weapons.

The Necessity of Bombing

To fully grasp why the bombings were deemed necessary, one must consider the broader context of the Pacific War and the United States' strategic objectives. Japan's military strategy was characterized by fierce resistance and a willingness to fight to the last man. The battles of Iwo Jima and Okinawa had demonstrated the high cost of invading Japanese-held territories, with both Allied and Japanese casualties reaching staggering numbers.

The United States sought to avoid a similarly protracted and bloody invasion of the Japanese mainland. The projected casualties for such an invasion were unacceptably high, and there was a desire to end the war swiftly to save lives on both sides. The atomic bomb, with its unprecedented destructive power, offered a means to compel Japan to surrender without the need for a costly and drawn-out invasion.

Furthermore, the geopolitical landscape played a crucial role in the decision. The United States wanted to assert its dominance and demonstrate its technological and military superiority, particularly to the Soviet Union. The successful use of the atomic bomb was intended to strengthen the United States' negotiating position in the post-war world and to discourage Soviet expansionism.

The Timing of the Second Bombing

The rapid succession of the bombings of Hiroshima and Nagasaki was a calculated decision. The United States wanted to maintain the psychological pressure on Japan, preventing any possibility of regrouping or resistance. The quick follow-up was intended to overwhelm Japan's leadership, compelling them to recognize the futility of continued resistance.

Moreover, the timing was influenced by logistical and operational considerations. The bombings were carried out as soon as the bombs and the bombers were ready, ensuring that the momentum of the shock and awe was maintained. Delaying the second bombing could have given Japan time to develop countermeasures or to evacuate key targets.

The Choice of Nagasaki

Nagasaki's selection as a target was influenced by a combination of strategic, tactical, and circumstantial factors. While it was not the primary target, its industrial and military significance made it a valuable target. The city's shipyards, steelworks, and arms factories were critical to Japan's war effort, and their destruction would significantly impair Japan's ability to continue the war.

Additionally, the geography of Nagasaki, with its valleys and hills, made it a challenging but effective target for demonstrating the bomb's power. The containment of the blast by the surrounding hills amplified the destruction within the city while providing a clear example of the bomb's effectiveness in different terrains.

The Broader Impact

The bombings of Hiroshima and Nagasaki had far-reaching implications that extended beyond the immediate end of World War II. They marked the beginning of the nuclear age, fundamentally altering the nature of warfare and international relations. The demonstration of the atomic bomb's power led to an arms race between the United States and the Soviet Union, shaping the geopolitical landscape of the Cold War.

The ethical and moral debates surrounding the use of atomic bombs on civilian populations continue to this day. The bombings raised profound questions about the principles of just war, the treatment of civilians, and the responsibilities of those who wield such destructive power.

The legacy of the bombings also includes the experiences of the hibakusha, who have become powerful advocates for peace and nuclear disarmament. Their testimonies have provided a human face to the abstract horrors of nuclear war, reminding the world of the catastrophic consequences of such weapons.

"Why Nagasaki?" is a journey through one of the most consequential events in modern history. It explores the complex interplay of military strategy, political decisions, technological advancements, and ethical considerations that led to the atomic bombings of Hiroshima and Nagasaki. Through detailed analysis and personal testimonies, this book seeks to understand why the bombings were deemed necessary, why a second bombing followed so swiftly, why Nagasaki was chosen as a target, and the scientific motivations behind using different bomb designs.

The story of Nagasaki is not just a tale of destruction; it is a testament to the resilience of the human spirit and the enduring quest for peace. It serves as a reminder of the profound impact of our decisions and the importance of learning from history to build a better future.

# CHAPTER ONE

# The Tokugawa Shogunate and the Impact of the Black Ships

The Rise of the Tokugawa Shogunate

In the early 17th century, Japan was a land divided by feuding warlords, each vying for control. Amidst this chaos emerged Tokugawa Ieyasu, a powerful leader who, after his victory at the Battle of Sekigahara in 1600, established a centralized feudal government in 1603. This government, known as the Tokugawa Shogunate, brought an end to the period of unrest known as the Sengoku (Warring States) period. Ieyasu became the shogun, or military ruler, ushering in a period of relative peace and stability known as the Edo period, which lasted for over 250 years.

Under the Tokugawa Shogunate, a rigid social hierarchy and centralized control were established. The emperor remained a figurehead in Kyoto, while real power resided with the shogun in Edo (modern-day Tokyo). The country was divided into domains ruled by daimyo (feudal lords), who were required to spend alternating years in Edo, a policy known as sankin-kotai (alternate attendance). This system helped prevent rebellion by keeping the daimyo under the watchful eye of the shogunate.

During the Edo period, Japan experienced economic growth, urbanization, and the development of a vibrant culture. Cities like

Edo, Osaka, and Kyoto became bustling centers of activity. The arts flourished, with kabuki theater, ukiyo-e woodblock prints, and haiku poetry gaining popularity. This period also saw the development of distinct Japanese cuisine, fashion, and social etiquette.

Isolationist Policy

To maintain control and prevent foreign influence, the Tokugawa Shogunate implemented a policy known as sakoku, or "closed country," in the 1630s. This policy severely restricted foreign trade and contact, allowing only the Dutch and Chinese limited trade through the port of Nagasaki. Japanese citizens were also forbidden from leaving the country. Despite these strict isolationist measures, the shogunate allowed a small number of Western books and scientific knowledge to enter Japan, leading to the development of rangaku (Dutch learning), which included studies in medicine, astronomy, and other sciences.

The Arrival of the Black Ships

In the mid-19th century, the United States, like other Western powers, sought to expand its trade and influence in Asia. In 1853, Commodore Matthew Perry arrived in Edo Bay (Tokyo Bay) with a squadron of four warships, known as the "Black Ships" due to their black hulls. Perry's mission was to open Japan to American trade and ensure the safety of shipwrecked American sailors.

The arrival of Perry's Black Ships was a shocking and intimidating display of Western military power. The Japanese were impressed by the advanced technology and firepower of Perry's steam-powered ships. Perry presented a letter from U.S. President Millard Fillmore, requesting the establishment of trade relations and better treatment of shipwrecked sailors. He then departed, promising to return for Japan's response.

Perry returned in 1854 with an even larger fleet, demonstrating that the United States was serious about its demands. Under pressure, the Tokugawa Shogunate signed the Treaty of Kanagawa on March 31, 1854. The treaty opened the ports of Shimoda and Hakodate to American ships, provided for the establishment of a U.S. consulate, and guaranteed the humane treatment of shipwrecked sailors.

Impact on Japan

The Treaty of Kanagawa marked the end of Japan's isolationist policy and opened the floodgates for other Western powers. Soon after, Britain, Russia, and the Netherlands secured similar treaties, leading to increased foreign presence and influence in Japan. The influx of foreign goods and ideas disrupted Japan's economy and social order. Traditional industries faced competition from Western imports, causing economic hardship for many artisans and merchants. The rigid social hierarchy of the Tokugawa era began to erode as new ideas about equality and modernization spread.

The shogunate's decision to open Japan to the West was deeply unpopular among many samurai and daimyo, who saw it as a betrayal of Japanese sovereignty. This dissatisfaction fueled political instability and opposition to the shogunate, leading to a period of turmoil known as the Bakumatsu (end of the shogunate). Nationalist sentiment and calls for reform grew stronger. Many young samurai, intellectuals, and merchants advocated for the restoration of imperial rule and the modernization of Japan to resist Western domination. The slogan "Sonno Joi" (Revere the Emperor, Expel the Barbarians) encapsulated these sentiments.

The Fall of the Tokugawa Shogunate

The growing opposition to the shogunate culminated in the Boshin War (1868-1869). Forces loyal to the Emperor, primarily from the domains of Satsuma and Choshu, clashed with shogunate forces. The conflict ended with the defeat of the shogunate and the restoration of imperial rule. On January 3, 1868, Emperor Meiji was declared the supreme ruler of Japan. The Meiji Restoration marked the end of the Tokugawa Shogunate and the beginning of a period of rapid modernization and reform. The new government abolished the feudal system, adopted Western technologies and institutions, and aimed to build a strong, centralized state.

Meiji Restoration: The Transformation of Japan

In the mid-19th century, Japan was a country firmly entrenched in feudal isolation under the Tokugawa shogunate. For over 250 years, the Tokugawa clan maintained strict control over the nation, enforcing a rigid social hierarchy and limiting foreign influence through a policy known as sakoku, or "closed country." Under this policy, Japan restricted trade to only a few ports and maintained minimal contact with the outside world, primarily through the Dutch and Chinese in Nagasaki. This isolation allowed Japan to enjoy a prolonged period of peace and stability, but it also meant that Japan lagged behind Western nations in terms of technological and military advancements.

The arrival of Commodore Matthew Perry's "Black Ships" in 1853 marked a turning point for Japan. Perry, representing the United States, arrived in Edo Bay (modern-day Tokyo Bay) with a squadron of steam-powered warships, demanding that Japan open its ports to American trade. The impressive display of Western naval power left the Japanese government with little choice. Faced with the superior firepower and technology of Perry's fleet, the Tokugawa shogunate agreed to sign the Treaty of Kanagawa in 1854, which opened two Japanese ports to American ships and established a U.S. consulate in Japan.

The signing of the Treaty of Kanagawa marked the end of Japan's isolationist policy and opened the country to increased foreign influence and trade. This sudden exposure to the outside world created economic and social upheaval. Traditional industries faced competition from Western imports, and new ideas about politics, society, and technology began to spread. The influx of foreign goods and ideas disrupted the established order and eroded the rigid social hierarchy that had defined the Tokugawa era.

Discontent with the shogunate's handling of foreign affairs and its inability to defend Japan's sovereignty grew among various social groups, particularly the samurai. Many samurai and daimyo (feudal lords) were outraged by the concessions made to foreign powers and the perceived weakness of the shogunate. This dissatisfaction fueled political instability and opposition to the shogunate, leading to the rise of nationalist and reformist movements. The slogan "Sonno Joi" (Revere the Emperor, Expel the Barbarians) captured the sentiment of these movements, which sought to restore imperial rule and modernize Japan to resist Western domination.

The political landscape of Japan became increasingly volatile as reformist and nationalist forces gained momentum. The shogunate's attempts to implement limited reforms were insufficient to quell the growing unrest. The Choshu and Satsuma domains, which had developed strong militaries and economies, became centers of opposition to the shogunate. These domains, along with other reformist groups, began to push for the restoration of imperial power and the modernization of Japan.

The tipping point came with the Boshin War, a civil war that erupted in 1868 between forces loyal to the Tokugawa shogunate and those supporting the restoration of imperial rule. The conflict began with the Battle of Toba-Fushimi, where the combined forces of Satsuma and Choshu defeated the shogunate's troops. The victory at Toba-Fushimi marked the beginning of the end for the Tokugawa shogunate. Faced with mounting military defeats and internal dissent, the last shogun, Tokugawa Yoshinobu, resigned, effectively ending the Tokugawa regime.

On January 3, 1868, Emperor Meiji was declared the supreme ruler of Japan, marking the official start of the Meiji Restoration. This period of transformation aimed to modernize Japan and restore power to the Emperor, who had been a symbolic figurehead under the Tokugawa shogunate. The new Meiji government set out to create a centralized state and implement widespread reforms to build a modern nation capable of standing up to Western powers.

One of the first steps taken by the Meiji government was the abolition of the feudal system. In 1871, the government replaced the feudal domains (han) with prefectures governed by centrally appointed officials. This move centralized power and laid the foundation for a modern administrative structure. The government also implemented land reforms, which redistributed land from the daimyo to the peasantry, weakening the traditional power of the feudal lords and fostering agricultural productivity.

To build a strong military capable of defending Japan and asserting its influence, the Meiji government introduced a conscript army based on the Prussian model. In 1873, they implemented universal conscription, requiring all able-bodied men to serve in the military. The navy was also modernized with the help of British advisors, and new technologies and training methods were adopted to create a formidable fighting force.

The Meiji leaders recognized that economic modernization was crucial for Japan's development. The government promoted industrialization through policies that encouraged the development of infrastructure such as railways, telegraph lines, and modern ports. They provided support for the establishment of factories and the adoption of Western technology. Key industries like textiles, shipbuilding, and mining received significant investment, leading to rapid industrial growth.

Education was another area of focus for the Meiji government. Understanding the importance of a well-educated population, they established a national education system and made elementary education compulsory. The government also founded universities and sent students abroad to learn Western sciences and technologies. The motto "Fukoku Kyohei" (Enrich the Country, Strengthen the Military) encapsulated the goal of using education to build a modern, powerful nation.

Legal and political reforms were also essential to the Meiji transformation. The government adopted Western legal codes and judicial practices to create a modern legal system. In 1889, the Meiji Constitution was promulgated, establishing a constitutional monarchy with an elected parliament (the Imperial Diet) and a cabinet responsible to the Emperor. These reforms laid the groundwork for a more democratic and participatory political system.

The cultural landscape of Japan also underwent significant changes during the Meiji era. Western influences permeated

Japanese society, leading to the adoption of Western dress, architecture, and customs, especially among the elite. At the same time, there was a strong emphasis on preserving and revitalizing traditional Japanese culture. This blend of old and new created a unique cultural identity for modern Japan.

The rapid modernization and reforms of the Meiji era were not without challenges. There was resistance from various social groups, particularly the samurai, who were unhappy about losing their privileged status and income. The Satsuma Rebellion of 1877, led by disaffected samurai under Saigo Takamori, was a notable example of this resistance. The rebellion was eventually crushed, reinforcing the government's authority and commitment to modernization.

By the early 20th century, Japan had transformed into a major industrial power. The Meiji era's emphasis on modernization and industrialization enabled Japan to compete with Western powers and pursue its own imperial ambitions. Japan's modernized military proved its effectiveness in conflicts such as the First Sino-Japanese War (1894-1895) and the Russo-Japanese War (1904-1905), establishing Japan as a formidable military power.

The Meiji Restoration laid the foundations for Japan's continued growth and development. The period fostered a spirit of innovation and adaptation that carried Japan through the challenges of the 20th century, including its rapid recovery and economic growth after World War II. The legacy of the Meiji Restoration is evident in Japan's continued emphasis on modernization, innovation, and the ability to blend tradition with progress, ensuring its prominent position in the world today.

# CHAPTER TWO

# The First Sino-Japanese War: A Turning Point in East Asia

In the late 19th century, the winds of change were sweeping across East Asia, stirring the longstanding equilibrium between China and Japan. For centuries, China, under the Qing Dynasty, had been the preeminent power in the region, its influence extending over Korea, which maintained a tributary relationship with the Middle Kingdom. Japan, emerging from over two centuries of isolation under the Tokugawa shogunate, was transforming rapidly through the Meiji Restoration.

Japan's transformation was nothing short of revolutionary. In 1868, Emperor Meiji ascended to the throne, marking the beginning of the Meiji era. Under his reign, Japan undertook an ambitious program of modernization and industrialization. The feudal system was dismantled, the samurai class was abolished, and the country was thrust into the industrial age. Railways, factories, and telegraph lines began to crisscross the landscape, and Western technology and educational systems were adopted to build a modern, cohesive state.

The driving force behind Japan's fervent modernization was a mix of national pride and a stark realization. The opening of Japan's ports by Commodore Perry's Black Ships in 1853 had exposed the country's vulnerability. Japanese leaders understood that to avoid the fate of other Asian nations succumbing to Western imperialism, Japan needed to match the West in military and economic power.

By the 1880s, Japan had built a formidable military. The new Imperial Japanese Army, trained and equipped with the latest technology, and the Imperial Japanese Navy, modeled after the British Royal Navy, were testaments to Japan's rapid progress. However, Japan's modernization was not solely for defense; it also harbored ambitions of expansion. The tiny island nation lacked natural resources, which were essential for its burgeoning industries. This scarcity drove Japan to look outward, particularly towards Korea and Manchuria, which were rich in resources and strategically significant.

Korea, at that time, was a hermit kingdom, resistant to outside influence and change. It was a vital interest for both China and Japan. For China, Korea served as a buffer state, protecting its northeastern borders. For Japan, Korea was seen as a dagger pointed at the heart of the homeland. Whoever controlled Korea could potentially threaten Japan.

The situation in Korea became increasingly unstable in the late 19th century. The Korean court was divided between factions favoring modernization and those wanting to maintain traditional isolation. The peasantry, suffering from poverty and corruption, was restless. The power vacuum and internal strife provided Japan with an opportunity to exert its influence.

In 1876, Japan forced Korea to sign the Treaty of Ganghwa, opening Korean ports to Japanese trade. This treaty was similar to those imposed on Japan by Western powers a few decades earlier. It marked the beginning of Japan's economic and political penetration into Korea. China, under the Qing Dynasty, was alarmed by Japan's growing influence but was preoccupied with internal problems and the pressures of Western imperialism.

The tension between Japan and China over Korea continued to mount. The tipping point came in 1894 with the Donghak Peasant Rebellion. This massive uprising, fueled by anti-government sentiment and calls for social reform, threatened to overthrow the Korean government. The Korean monarchy, unable to quell the rebellion, requested military assistance from China. Following the Convention of Tientsin, which required both Japan and China to notify each other before sending troops to Korea, China informed Japan of its intervention.

Japan saw China's intervention as a direct threat to its interests. The Meiji government decided to act. Japanese troops were dispatched to Korea under the pretext of protecting Japanese nationals and restoring order. However, Japan's true intention was to assert its dominance over Korea and challenge Chinese influence.

The clash became inevitable. In July 1894, tensions escalated when a Japanese warship sank the Kow-shing, a British transport ship carrying Chinese troops. This incident marked the beginning of open hostilities between Japan and China. Both nations formally declared war on August 1, 1894.

The First Sino-Japanese War was not merely a conflict between two nations but a clash of two different eras. China, with its ancient traditions and vast empire, faced a newly awakened Japan, eager to prove its place among the modern powers. The war would demonstrate the effectiveness of Japan's modernization efforts and signal a shift in the balance of power in East Asia.

As Japanese forces moved swiftly and decisively, the weaknesses of the Qing Dynasty became evident. China's military, plagued by outdated strategies, corruption, and internal strife, was ill-prepared for the modernized and highly motivated Japanese forces. The war unfolded with a series of Japanese victories, each further eroding Chinese control over Korea and Manchuria.

The background of the First Sino-Japanese War is a story of ambition, transformation, and the inevitable clash that arises when an emerging power seeks to reshape the established order. It highlights the complexities of international relations and the impact of internal reforms on a nation's ability to project power on the global stage. The war would not only change the fate of Korea but also herald Japan's rise as a dominant force in East Asia, setting the stage for future conflicts and the continued struggle for influence in the region.

The war marked a significant shift in the balance of power in East Asia. Japan emerged as a major regional power, demonstrating its military prowess and modern capabilities. In contrast, China's defeat exposed the weaknesses of the Qing Dynasty and its inability to modernize effectively.

Japan's victory fueled national pride and justified the country's modernization efforts. The government and military continued to modernize, further strengthening Japan's position on the global stage. In China, the defeat humiliated the Qing Dynasty, exacerbating internal strife and contributing to the rise of revolutionary movements. The war's outcome underscored the need for significant reforms, leading to the Self-Strengthening Movement and other modernization efforts, albeit with limited success.

Shortly after the Treaty of Shimonoseki, Russia, Germany, and France intervened, forcing Japan to return the Liaodong Peninsula to China in exchange for additional indemnity. This intervention revealed the complexities of international diplomacy and the rivalries among Western powers in East Asia.

The war set the stage for future conflicts, including the Russo-Japanese War (1904-1905), as Japan continued its expansionist policies. It also contributed to the eventual downfall of the Qing Dynasty and the rise of the Republic of China in 1912.

The First Sino-Japanese War was a pivotal event that reshaped East Asia. Japan's decisive victory demonstrated the effectiveness of its modernization efforts and established it as a dominant regional power. For China, the defeat highlighted the urgent need for reform and modernization but also led to greater internal instability. The war's legacy influenced the geopolitical dynamics of the region for decades to come, setting the stage for future conflicts and transformations.

# CHAPTER THREE

# The Second Sino-Japanese War: A Saga of Struggle and Transformation

Prelude to Conflict

In the early 20<sup>th</sup> century, the world was in turmoil. The First World War had reshaped national boundaries and left deep scars on the international order. Amidst this global upheaval, East Asia was a region of intense rivalry and strategic significance. China, under the rule of the weakened Qing Dynasty, was grappling with internal strife and external threats. Meanwhile, Japan, having undergone rapid modernization and industrialization during the Meiji Restoration, was emerging as a formidable military power with expansionist ambitions.

China, transitioning from the Qing Dynasty to the Republic of China after the 1911 revolution, found itself beset by warlordism and political fragmentation. The Nationalist Party (Kuomintang or KMT) under Chiang Kai-shek sought to unify the country and resist foreign encroachments. However, internal conflicts, particularly with the Communist Party of China (CPC) led by Mao Zedong, sapped China's strength and made it vulnerable to external threats.

Japan, on the other hand, had consolidated its power and sought to extend its influence in Asia. The victory in the Russo-Japanese War (1904-1905) and the annexation of Korea in 1910 emboldened

Japanese imperial ambitions. The Japanese military, driven by a desire for resources and strategic dominance, viewed China as both a threat and an opportunity. The Mukden Incident of 1931, orchestrated by the Japanese army, led to the invasion of Manchuria and the establishment of the puppet state of Manchukuo. This act of aggression was condemned internationally, but effective opposition was lacking.

The Road to War

The early 1930s saw growing tensions between Japan and China. Japan's aggressive policies and actions, such as the occupation of Manchuria, were met with Chinese resistance and international disapproval. The League of Nations condemned Japan's actions, but Japan withdrew from the organization, indicating its unwillingness to abide by international norms.

By the mid-1930s, Japan had intensified its efforts to expand its influence in China. The signing of the Anti-Comintern Pact with Germany in 1936 further aligned Japan with fascist powers, heightening the threat it posed to China. In July 1937, a seemingly minor skirmish between Japanese and Chinese troops at the Marco Polo Bridge near Beijing escalated into a full-scale conflict. The Marco Polo Bridge Incident marked the official start of the Second Sino-Japanese War.

The Outbreak of War

The Japanese strategy was to rapidly overwhelm Chinese forces through a series of coordinated assaults. Japanese troops, well-equipped and disciplined, quickly captured key cities such as Beijing and Tianjin. The Chinese Nationalist government, determined to resist, moved its capital from Nanjing to Chongqing to continue the fight from the interior.

The Battle of Shanghai, which began in August 1937, was one of the early and significant confrontations of the war. Japanese forces launched a massive assault on Shanghai, one of China's most important economic and cultural centers. The battle lasted three months and involved intense urban combat, resulting in heavy casualties on both sides. Despite fierce resistance, Shanghai fell to the Japanese in November 1937.

Following the fall of Shanghai, Japanese forces advanced towards Nanjing, the Chinese capital at the time. The capture of Nanjing in December 1937 led to one of the most infamous atrocities of the war, known as the Nanjing Massacre or the Rape of Nanjing. Japanese troops committed widespread atrocities, including mass executions, rapes, and looting. An estimated 200,000 to 300,000 Chinese civilians and disarmed soldiers were killed. The brutality of the massacre shocked the world and deepened Chinese resolve to resist Japanese aggression.

Stalemate and Resistance

Despite the early Japanese successes, the war soon reached a stalemate. China, vast and populous, proved difficult to subdue. The Chinese government relocated to Chongqing, from where it continued to coordinate resistance efforts. The mountainous terrain of the interior provided natural defences against Japanese advances.

Chinese resistance was multifaceted. The Nationalist government led by Chiang Kai-shek maintained conventional military operations, while the Communist forces under Mao Zedong engaged in extensive guerrilla warfare. The Communists, operating primarily in rural areas, built strong support networks among the peasantry and conducted sabotage operations to disrupt Japanese supply lines. This dual approach of conventional and guerrilla warfare created a persistent challenge for the Japanese occupiers.

International Involvement and Escalation

The Second Sino-Japanese War did not occur in isolation; it was deeply intertwined with the broader context of global geopolitics and the emerging conflict of World War II. China received varying degrees of support from international actors. The Soviet Union provided military aid and advisors to the Chinese Nationalists, motivated by a desire to counter Japanese expansionism and protect its own interests in the region. The United States, while initially maintaining a policy of neutrality, gradually increased its support for China through economic assistance and the sale of military supplies.

The global conflict reached a turning point with Japan's attack on Pearl Harbor on December 7, 1941. This attack brought the United States into World War II and marked the beginning of the Pacific War. The Second Sino-Japanese War became part of the larger conflict, with China officially joining the Allies against the Axis powers. The United States extended significant aid to China through the Lend-Lease program, which provided military equipment and supplies crucial for sustaining the Chinese war effort.

Japanese Strategy and Brutality

Japan's strategy in China involved a combination of direct military assaults and brutal tactics aimed at terrorizing the population into submission. The policy known as "Three Alls" (Kill All, Burn All, Loot All) exemplified this approach. Japanese forces committed numerous atrocities, including the use of biological warfare conducted by Unit 731. These actions inflicted immense suffering on the Chinese population and fueled widespread hatred and resistance against the Japanese occupiers.

Turning Points and Allied Victory

Several key battles and campaigns marked turning points in the war. The Battle of Changsha, fought in three major engagements between 1939 and 1942, saw Chinese forces successfully repel Japanese offensives, boosting Chinese morale and demonstrating their ability to resist. The strategic importance of Changsha, a major transportation hub, made these victories significant.

The Burma Road, a vital supply route connecting British-held Burma with China, played a crucial role in sustaining Chinese resistance. Despite Japanese efforts to cut off this lifeline, the Allies managed to keep the road open, ensuring a steady flow of supplies and aid to Chinese forces.

By 1944, Japan was overextended on multiple fronts. The United States and its Allies launched successful campaigns in the Pacific, pushing Japanese forces back and reclaiming occupied territories.

The Japanese military, stretched thin and facing increasing pressure, struggled to maintain its hold on China.

Operation Ichi-Go, launched by Japan in 1944, aimed to secure a continuous land route from Manchuria to Southeast Asia and consolidate Japanese control over central China. Although initially successful, the operation ultimately failed to achieve its strategic objectives and further strained Japanese resources.

Consequences and Legacy

The Second Sino-Japanese War had profound and far-reaching consequences for China, Japan, and the world. The war resulted in immense human suffering and loss. It is estimated that 15 to 20 million Chinese died, including both military personnel and civilians. The war caused widespread destruction of infrastructure, cities, and farmlands, leaving China economically crippled and deeply scarred.

The political landscape of China was significantly altered by the war. The Nationalists, weakened by corruption and military losses, struggled to maintain control. Meanwhile, the Communists, who had gained popular support through their resistance efforts and promises of land reform, emerged as a formidable force. The uneasy alliance between the Nationalists and Communists during the war collapsed shortly after Japan's surrender, leading to the resumption of the Chinese Civil War. The Communists, led by Mao Zedong, eventually emerged victorious in 1949, establishing the People's Republic of China. The Nationalists retreated to Taiwan, where they established the Republic of China.

The war also had a lasting impact on Sino-Japanese relations. The atrocities committed during the conflict, particularly the Nanjing Massacre, left a deep scar on Chinese national consciousness and fueled long-standing animosity towards Japan. Historical grievances and territorial disputes continue to affect diplomatic relations between the two nations to this day.

On a global scale, the Second Sino-Japanese War was a significant precursor to World War II in the Pacific and had lasting implications for international relations. The conflict highlighted the dangers of aggressive expansionism and the importance of international cooperation to maintain peace. The war also underscored the necessity for a global framework to address and prevent atrocities, leading to the establishment of institutions such as the United Nations.

The war's legacy influenced the geopolitical dynamics of East Asia and the world. Japan, defeated and devastated, underwent a period of American occupation and extensive reforms. Under the guidance of General Douglas MacArthur, Japan adopted a new constitution, embraced democratic governance, and demilitarized. These reforms laid the foundation for Japan's post-war recovery and transformation into a pacifist and economically prosperous nation.

China, emerging from the war and subsequent civil conflict, faced the monumental task of reconstruction and nation-building. The Communist victory led to the establishment of a socialist state under Mao Zedong, with far-reaching social and economic reforms. The People's Republic of China embarked on a path of industrialization and modernization, eventually becoming a major global power.

In conclusion, the Second Sino-Japanese War was a brutal and transformative conflict that reshaped East Asia and had profound implications for global geopolitics. The war demonstrated the resilience of the Chinese people and the complexities of wartime alliances. Its legacy continues to influence regional dynamics and historical memory, underscoring the importance of understanding this pivotal period in history to comprehend the broader context of World War II and the subsequent development of modern Asia.

# CHAPTER FOUR

# The "Three Alls" Policy: A Dark Chapter in the Second Sino-Japanese War

In the midst of the brutal Second Sino-Japanese War, the Japanese Imperial Army adopted a scorched-earth strategy known as the "Three Alls" policy, or "Sankō Sakusen" in Japanese. This policy, which translates to "Kill All, Burn All, Loot All," was aimed at crushing Chinese resistance through terror and complete devastation. The origins of this policy can be traced to the early years of the conflict, as Japanese forces faced fierce guerrilla resistance from Chinese troops and civilians alike.

By 1940, the Japanese military found itself bogged down in a protracted war that seemed to have no end in sight. Conventional military tactics had proven insufficient to subdue the vast and populous Chinese mainland. Guerrilla warfare, conducted primarily by the Chinese Communist forces under Mao Zedong, inflicted significant casualties on Japanese troops and disrupted their supply lines. The Japanese high command, frustrated and desperate for a decisive solution, turned to the "Three Alls" policy as a means of breaking the will of the Chinese people and cutting off support for the guerrillas.

The "Three Alls" policy was formally initiated in 1942, under the command of General Yasuji Okamura, who was tasked with implementing the strategy across northern China. The policy called for the complete annihilation of any village or community suspected of harbouring or supporting Chinese resistance fighters. Japanese troops were ordered to kill all inhabitants, burn all structures, and loot all resources, leaving nothing behind that could be of use to the enemy.

The execution of this policy was brutal and systematic. Japanese soldiers, already hardened by years of intense combat, carried out their orders with ruthless efficiency. Villages were surrounded, and their inhabitants were subjected to indiscriminate slaughter. Homes, schools, and temples were set ablaze, and anything of value was seized or destroyed. The goal was to create a wasteland devoid of life and resources, thereby denying the guerrillas any support base.

The impact of the "Three Alls" policy on the Chinese civilian population was catastrophic. Entire communities were wiped out, and countless innocent lives were lost. Families were torn apart, and survivors were left to wander through the ashes of their former homes, searching for remnants of their lives amid the ruins. The psychological trauma inflicted by these atrocities left deep scars on the Chinese people, fostering a burning hatred for the Japanese invaders.

One particularly harrowing account comes from the village of Panjiayu, in Hebei Province. In January 1941, Japanese forces surrounded the village as part of a "mopping-up" operation. The soldiers went from house to house, dragging out men, women, and children, and summarily executing them. The village was then set on fire, and all livestock and crops were seized or destroyed. Out of a population of over 1,200, fewer than 300 survived. Panjiayu became a symbol of the horrors of the "Three Alls" policy and the resilience of the Chinese spirit in the face of unimaginable suffering.

Despite the overwhelming brutality of the "Three Alls" policy, Chinese resistance did not falter. In fact, the policy often had the opposite effect of what the Japanese intended. Instead of breaking the will of the Chinese people, it galvanized them. The atrocities committed by the Japanese army fueled anti-Japanese sentiment and strengthened the resolve of the resistance fighters.

The Chinese Communist Party, adept at guerrilla warfare, used the atrocities to rally support among the peasantry. They highlighted the brutality of the Japanese and the suffering of the Chinese people to recruit more fighters and garner greater support from the civilian population. Propaganda leaflets and broadcasts detailed the horrors of the "Three Alls" policy, urging people to join the resistance and fight for their homeland.

The Nationalist forces under Chiang Kai-shek also condemned the Japanese actions and called for international support. Reports of the atrocities reached the global stage, drawing condemnation from other nations and increasing sympathy for the Chinese cause. Although the international community was largely preoccupied with the broader conflict of World War II, the plight of the Chinese people under Japanese occupation could not be entirely ignored.

Long-term Consequences

The "Three Alls" policy, while intended to crush Chinese resistance, ultimately contributed to Japan's defeat. The widespread atrocities alienated the Japanese from the Chinese population and undermined any attempts to gain local support. The policy also intensified international condemnation of Japanese aggression, adding to the global resolve to defeat Japan.

After Japan's surrender in 1945, the full extent of the atrocities committed under the "Three Alls" policy came to light. War crimes tribunals were held, and many Japanese military leaders were held accountable for their actions. General Yasuji Okamura, the architect of the policy, was tried for war crimes but controversially received a lighter sentence due to his cooperation with the Allies during the post-war occupation of Japan.

The legacy of the "Three Alls" policy remains a painful chapter in the history of Sino-Japanese relations. The atrocities committed during this period left a deep and lasting impact on the collective memory of the Chinese people. The memories of the suffering endured and the resilience shown continue to shape the national identity and historical consciousness of China.

Global Geopolitical Impact

The Second Sino-Japanese War, and the "Three Alls" policy in particular, had significant implications for global geopolitics. The war highlighted the dangers of unchecked militarism and expansionism, influencing the post-war international order and the establishment of institutions aimed at preventing such atrocities.

The war also had a profound impact on the balance of power in East Asia. Japan's defeat and subsequent occupation by the Allied powers led to a period of reconstruction and reform. The demilitarization and democratization of Japan, guided by the United States, transformed the country into a pacifist and economically prosperous nation. This transformation laid the foundation for Japan's post-war recovery and its emergence as a key ally of the United States during the Cold War.

In China, the end of the war marked the resumption of the civil conflict between the Nationalists and Communists. The Communist victory in 1949 and the establishment of the People's Republic of China reshaped the geopolitical landscape of East Asia. The rise of Communist China as a major global power had far-reaching implications for international relations and the ideological struggle between the capitalist West and the communist East.

The legacy of the Second Sino-Japanese War and the "Three Alls" policy continues to influence contemporary geopolitics. Historical grievances and unresolved territorial disputes remain sources of tension between China and Japan. Efforts to foster reconciliation and mutual understanding are ongoing, but the shadow of the past still looms large over bilateral relations.

In conclusion, the "Three Alls" policy was a dark and tragic chapter in the history of the Second Sino-Japanese War. The policy's brutality and the suffering it caused left an indelible mark on the Chinese people and had significant geopolitical repercussions. Understanding this period is essential for comprehending the complexities of Sino-Japanese relations and the broader impact of the war on global geopolitics. The resilience and determination of the Chinese people in the face of such atrocities stand as a testament to the enduring human spirit and the quest for justice and peace.

# Russo-Japanese War: A Clash of Empires-The Second Russo-Japanese War

Russo-Japanese War: A Clash of Empires-The Second Russo-Japanese War

In the dawn of the 20<sup>th</sup> century, East Asia was a cauldron of imperial ambitions and nationalist fervour. The First Russo-Japanese War, fought between 1904 and 1905, had already reshaped the balance of power in the region, marking the first significant victory of an Asian power over a European one. Japan's triumph had not only established it as a formidable force but had also ignited a surge of nationalism and modernization throughout Asia.

However, the seeds of further conflict were sown in the turbulent decades that followed. Both Japan and Russia harboured unresolved ambitions and grievances. As the world edged closer to the cataclysm of World War II, these two powers would again find themselves on a collision course. The Second Russo-Japanese War, though often overshadowed by the broader global conflict, was a crucial chapter in the struggle for dominance in East Asia and had profound implications for world geopolitics.

The Interwar Period: Rising Tensions

After their defeat in 1905, the Russian Empire underwent significant political and social upheaval. The loss to Japan exposed the weaknesses of the Tsarist regime and contributed to the revolutionary fervor that culminated in the Bolshevik Revolution of 1917. The new Soviet Union, under the leadership of Vladimir Lenin and later Joseph Stalin, sought to rebuild and strengthen its position both domestically and internationally.

Meanwhile, Japan capitalized on its victory and continued its path of industrialization and militarization. The Meiji Restoration had transformed Japan into a modern state, and its leaders were determined to expand their empire. Japan's occupation of Korea in 1910 and its incursions into China in the 1930s were steps toward establishing dominance in East Asia.

The interwar period saw a series of border skirmishes and conflicts between the Soviet Union and Japan, particularly in Manchuria. The most notable of these was the Battle of Khalkhin Gol in 1939, where Soviet forces, led by General Georgy Zhukov, decisively defeated the Japanese. This conflict was a prelude to the larger confrontation that would come with the onset of World War II.

World War II and the Brewing Conflict

As World War II engulfed the globe, Japan and the Soviet Union initially maintained a tense neutrality toward each other, formalized by the Soviet-Japanese Neutrality Pact of 1941. This agreement allowed the Soviet Union to focus on the war in Europe, while Japan concentrated on its campaigns in the Pacific and Southeast Asia.

However, the dynamic began to shift as the war progressed. The United States, seeking to weaken Japan's war effort, urged the Soviet Union to join the Allies in the fight against Japan. Stalin, while cautious, recognized the strategic advantage of striking Japan at an opportune moment to reclaim lost territories and expand Soviet influence in Asia.

The Turning Point: In February 1945, the Yalta Conference brought together the leaders of the Allied powers: President Franklin D. Roosevelt of the United States, Prime Minister Winston Churchill of the United Kingdom, and Premier Joseph Stalin of the Soviet Union. One of the critical discussions at Yalta was the Soviet Union's entry into the war against Japan.

Stalin agreed to enter the war against Japan within three months of Germany's defeat. In return, the Allies promised several territorial concessions to the Soviet Union, including the return of southern Sakhalin and the Kuril Islands, which had been lost to Japan in the First Russo-Japanese War. The stage was set for a renewed conflict between the Soviet Union and Japan.

EnteThe "Big Three" at the Yalta Conference, Winston Churchill, Franklin D. Roosevelt and Joseph Stalin. Behind them stand,sov.(Wikipedia) from the left, Field Marshal Sir Alan Brooke, Fleet Admiral Ernest King, Fleet Admiral William D. Leahy, General of the Army George Marshall, Major General Laurence S. Kuter, General Aleksei Antonov, Vice Admiral Stepan Kucherov, and Admiral of the Fleet Nikolay Kuznetr Caption

The Outbreak of the Second Russo-Japanese War

Germany's surrender on May 8, 1945, set the countdown for the Soviet Union's entry into the Pacific War. On August 8, 1945, just two days after the atomic bombing of Hiroshima, the Soviet Union declared war on Japan. The following day, Soviet forces launched a massive offensive into Japanese-held territories in Manchuria, known as the Manchurian Strategic Offensive Operation.

The Soviet invasion was a masterclass in military strategy and execution. Marshal Aleksandr Vasilevsky, commanding the Soviet forces, orchestrated a multi-pronged assault involving over 1.5 million troops, supported by thousands of tanks, aircraft, and artillery pieces. The Japanese Kwantung Army, though sizable, was ill-prepared and poorly equipped to face such a formidable force.

The Invasion of Manchuria

The Soviet offensive was swift and overwhelming. Utilizing deep battle tactics and blitzkrieg-style manoeuvres, Soviet forces rapidly advanced into Manchuria, encircling and destroying Japanese units. Key cities and strategic points fell with alarming speed, and the Japanese defenders were thrown into disarray.

The city of Harbin, a major industrial and administrative center, was one of the first to fall. Soviet paratroopers and armoured divisions struck with precision, overwhelming the Japanese garrison. The capture of Harbin severed critical supply lines and further demoralized Japanese forces.

In the south, Soviet troops crossed the Amur River and advanced into the Korean Peninsula, aiming to liberate Korea from Japanese occupation. The Korean people, long suffering under Japanese rule, welcomed the Soviet forces as liberators, although the future political landscape of Korea would soon become a contentious issue.

The Fall of Sakhalin and the Kurils

Simultaneously, Soviet forces launched amphibious assaults on southern Sakhalin and the Kuril Islands. The Japanese defenders, though determined, were no match for the Soviet onslaught. The capture of these territories not only fulfilled the promises made at Yalta but also provided the Soviet Union with strategic footholds in the Pacific.

The Kuril Islands, in particular, became a point of geopolitical significance. Their location provided the Soviet Union with control over the Sea of Okhotsk and enhanced its strategic depth against any future conflicts in the Pacific. The islands would remain a contentious issue between Japan and Russia for decades to come.

Japan's Surrender and the End of the War

The Soviet invasion, combined with the devastating atomic bombings of Hiroshima and Nagasaki, shattered Japan's ability to continue the war. On August 15, 1945, Emperor Hirohito announced Japan's surrender in a radio broadcast, marking the end of World War II. The formal surrender documents were signed aboard the USS Missouri on September 2, 1945.

The Soviet Union's swift and decisive campaign in Manchuria played a crucial role in compelling Japan's surrender. The collapse of the Japanese Kwantung Army and the loss of key territories eliminated any remaining hope for Japan to negotiate better terms or continue the fight.

Impact on World Geopolitics

The Second Russo-Japanese War had profound implications for world geopolitics and the post-war order in East Asia.

1. The Emergence of the Cold War

The end of World War II marked the beginning of the Cold War, a period of intense rivalry between the Soviet Union and the United States. The Soviet invasion of Manchuria and the subsequent occupation of northern Korea laid the groundwork for future geopolitical tensions in the region.

In Korea, the Soviet Union and the United States agreed to divide the peninsula along the 38$^{th}$ parallel, with the Soviets occupying the north and the Americans the south. This division eventually led to the establishment of two separate states: the communist North Korea and the capitalist South Korea. The Korean Peninsula would become a flashpoint in the Cold War, culminating in the Korean War from 1950 to 1953.

2. The Redrawing of Borders

The territorial changes resulting from the Second Russo-Japanese War had lasting effects on the geopolitical landscape of East Asia. The Soviet Union's acquisition of southern Sakhalin and the Kuril Islands solidified its presence in the Pacific and enhanced its strategic position against Japan and other potential adversaries.

The loss of these territories was a significant blow to Japan, contributing to its post-war identity and territorial disputes. The Kuril Islands dispute remains unresolved, with Japan continuing to claim sovereignty over the northernmost islands, known as the Northern Territories in Japan.

3. The Rise of Communist China

The Soviet invasion of Manchuria also had a profound impact on China. The Japanese occupation had weakened the Nationalist government of Chiang Kai-shek, while the Communist forces under Mao Zedong had strengthened their position through guerrilla warfare and popular support.

The Soviet presence in Manchuria provided the Chinese Communists with access to captured Japanese weapons and resources, bolstering their capabilities. The subsequent Chinese Civil War saw the Communists emerge victorious, establishing the People's Republic of China in 1949. The rise of Communist China reshaped the political landscape of Asia and significantly influenced the global balance of power during the Cold War.

4. The U.S.-Japan Alliance

The end of World War II marked the beginning of a new relationship between the United States and Japan. Under the guidance of General Douglas MacArthur, Japan underwent a period of occupation and reconstruction. The United States implemented significant political, economic, and social reforms, transforming Japan into a democratic and pacifist nation.

The U.S.-Japan Security Treaty, signed in 1951, established a strong military alliance between the two countries. The United States guaranteed Japan's security, and in return, Japan allowed the stationing of U.S. forces on its territory. This alliance became a cornerstone of U.S. strategy in Asia during the Cold War and remains a key element of regional security to this day.

5. The Soviet Union's Strategic Gains

The Soviet Union's successful campaign in Manchuria and its territorial acquisitions enhanced its strategic position in the Pacific and East Asia. The presence of Soviet forces in the region provided a counterbalance to U.S. influence and established the Soviet Union as a major player in Asian geopolitics.

The Soviet Union's actions also demonstrated its military prowess and ability to project power beyond its immediate borders. This contributed to the perception of the Soviet Union as a global superpower and shaped the strategic calculations of both the United States and its allies during the early years of the Cold War.

The Legacy of the Second Russo-Japanese War

The Second Russo-Japanese War, though overshadowed by the broader context of World War II, was a significant conflict with far-reaching consequences. It reshaped the geopolitical landscape of East Asia, contributed to the onset of the Cold War, and influenced the strategic decisions of major powers for decades to come.

The war also highlighted the complexities of post-war reconstruction and the challenges of establishing a stable and lasting peace. The unresolved territorial disputes, ideological conflicts, and power struggles that emerged from the war continue to shape the dynamics of international relations in the region.

As we reflect on the Second Russo-Japanese War, it serves as a reminder of the intricate interplay between military strategy, political ambition, and the quest for power. The decisions made during this period reverberate through history, shaping the world we live in today. Understanding this conflict provides valuable insights into the broader narrative of 20th-century geopolitics and the ongoing quest for stability and security in East Asia.

# CHAPTER SIX

# Reasons for Japan Aligning with the Axis Powers Instead of the Allied Force -The Rising Sun: Japan's Path to the Axis Powers

The Dawn of Ambition

In the dawn of the 20th century, Japan stood at a crossroads. The Meiji Restoration had transformed the nation from a feudal society into a burgeoning industrial power. Japan's rapid modernization and military victories over China in 1895 and Russia in 1905 marked its emergence as a formidable force in East Asia. Yet, Japan's meteoric rise also sowed the seeds of future conflict, as its ambitions clashed with those of Western powers.

The Quest for Resources

Japan's geographic isolation and limited natural resources presented significant challenges for its industrial economy. As the nation modernized, the need for raw materials such as coal, iron, and oil became increasingly pressing. Domestic resources were insufficient, compelling Japan to look abroad.

The First Sino-Japanese War (1894-1895) and the subsequent acquisition of Taiwan marked the beginning of Japan's imperial expansion. This was followed by the Russo-Japanese War (1904-1905), where Japan's victory over a European power astonished the world and solidified its status as a major military power. The Treaty of Portsmouth, which ended the war, granted Japan control over Korea and Southern Manchuria, providing access to valuable resources and strategic territories.

The Korean Peninsula and Manchuria

Korea, annexed by Japan in 1910, became a crucial part of Japan's empire, serving as a gateway to the Asian mainland. Manchuria, with its vast resources and strategic location, was particularly attractive. The Mukden Incident in 1931, orchestrated by the Japanese military, provided a pretext for the invasion of Manchuria and the establishment of the puppet state of Manchukuo.

The occupation of Manchuria demonstrated Japan's willingness to use military force to secure its interests, highlighting the growing rift between Japan and the Western powers. The League of Nations condemned Japan's actions, leading to Japan's withdrawal from the organization. This diplomatic isolation pushed Japan further towards seeking alliances with other revisionist powers.

The Economic Strain of Expansion

The costs of maintaining and expanding an empire placed a significant strain on Japan's economy. Military expenditures soared, and the need for resources intensified. The global economic depression of the 1930s exacerbated these challenges, as international trade declined and competition for resources increased.

In response, Japan pursued a policy of economic self-sufficiency through territorial expansion. The concept of the "Greater East Asia Co-Prosperity Sphere" was developed, envisioning a bloc of Asian nations led by Japan and free from Western colonial influence. This vision of regional dominance would become a cornerstone of Japan's foreign policy and drive its quest for new alliances.

The Rise of Anti-Western Sentiment-Cultural Clashes and Humiliations

Japan's encounters with Western powers were often fraught with tension and humiliation. The forced opening of Japan's ports by Commodore Perry's Black Ships in 1853 was a stark reminder of Western superiority and Japan's vulnerability. The subsequent unequal treaties imposed by Western powers further deepened this sense of humiliation.

The early 20$^{th}$ century saw Japan striving to assert itself as an equal among the Western powers, yet facing persistent discrimination. Despite Japan's significant contributions to the Allied efforts in World War I, the Treaty of Versailles in 1919 did not grant Japan the territorial gains it sought, and the Western powers dismissed Japan's proposal for racial equality. These slights fueled resentment and a desire to overturn the existing international order.

The Impact of Western Imperialism

The expansion of Western colonial empires in Asia and the Pacific was viewed with growing alarm in Japan. The Western powers, particularly Britain, France, and the United States, controlled vast territories and resources. Japan, by contrast, was a latecomer to imperialism and faced fierce competition for colonies.

The Western powers' dominance in China, exemplified by the treaty ports and spheres of influence, was particularly galling. The 1924 Immigration Act in the United States, which effectively banned Japanese immigration, further inflamed anti-Western sentiment. Many Japanese saw these actions as evidence of Western hypocrisy and racism, reinforcing the belief that Japan needed to assert itself militarily to secure its interests.

The Influence of Nationalism and Militarism

The rise of nationalism and militarism in Japan during the 1930s was closely linked to anti-Western sentiment. Nationalist ideologues promoted the idea of Japan's unique destiny and superiority, emphasizing the need to liberate Asia from Western colonial rule. The military, increasingly influential in politics, saw

Western powers as both a threat and an obstacle to Japan's ambitions.

Organizations such as the Imperial Rule Assistance Association and ultranationalist groups like the Black Dragon Society advocated for a strong, militarized Japan capable of standing up to the West. The assassination of Prime Minister Inukai Tsuyoshi in 1932 marked a turning point, signalling the decline of civilian government and the ascendancy of the military.

Diplomatic Manoeuvres and Ideological Alignment-Germany's Influence

The rise of Adolf Hitler and the Nazi Party in Germany had a profound impact on Japan's strategic thinking. Hitler's vision of a New Order in Europe, based on the principles of racial purity and territorial expansion, resonated with the Japanese military's own goals of creating a hierarchical order in Asia.

Diplomatic contacts between Japan and Germany increased during the 1930s. Both nations shared a common disdain for the existing international order and sought to challenge the dominance of the Western powers. The Anti-Comintern Pact, signed by Japan and Germany in 1936, formalized their opposition to the spread of communism and laid the groundwork for closer military cooperation.

The Rome-Berlin-Tokyo Axis

The Anti-Comintern Pact was soon joined by Italy, under the fascist regime of Benito Mussolini. This tripartite alliance, known as the Rome-Berlin-Tokyo Axis, was driven by mutual interests and ideological affinities. All three nations sought to revise the status quo and expand their empires.

For Japan, the alliance with Germany and Italy offered several advantages. It provided a counterbalance to the influence of the United States and the British Empire in Asia, offered potential military and technological cooperation, and reinforced Japan's position as a major power on the global stage.

The Road to War

The Second Sino-Japanese War, which began in 1937, was a brutal and protracted conflict that further strained Japan's resources and intensified its search for allies. Despite initial successes, Japanese forces encountered fierce resistance from Chinese Nationalist and Communist troops. The conflict bogged down into a war of attrition, with devastating consequences for both sides. Japan's brutal tactics, including the infamous Nanjing Massacre, drew international condemnation but also highlighted the need for a decisive strategy to secure victory.

Strategic Calculations and Alliances-The Search for Resources

The protracted war in China heightened Japan's desperation for resources. The United States, concerned about Japanese aggression, imposed economic sanctions, including embargoes on oil and other critical materials. These sanctions threatened to cripple Japan's war effort and economy.

Faced with the prospect of economic strangulation, Japan's leaders debated their options. Some advocated for a diplomatic resolution, but the prevailing sentiment within the military was that Japan must secure its own resources through further territorial expansion. This led to the decision to seize the resource-rich territories of Southeast Asia, which were under the control of European colonial powers.

The Decision to Strike

Japan's leaders understood that any move to seize Southeast Asia would likely provoke a response from the United States. The attack on Pearl Harbor, planned meticulously by Admiral Isoroku Yamamoto, was intended to neutralize the U.S. Pacific Fleet and buy Japan time to consolidate its gains.

On December 7, 1941, Japan launched a surprise attack on Pearl Harbor, devastating the U.S. fleet and bringing the United States into World War II. Simultaneously, Japanese forces launched offensives across Southeast Asia, quickly capturing key territories such as the Philippines, Malaya, and the Dutch East Indies.

The Impact of the Alliance-The Early Victories

In the early years of the Pacific War, Japan's alliance with the Axis Powers seemed to pay dividends. The Japanese military achieved a series of stunning victories, rapidly expanding its empire and securing critical resources. The fall of Singapore, the capture of the Philippines, and the conquest of the Dutch East Indies demonstrated Japan's military prowess.

The strategic coordination with Germany and Italy also posed a significant challenge to the Allied powers. The Axis powers' ability to threaten multiple fronts forced the Allies to spread their resources thin and complicated their strategic planning.

The Turning Tide

However, the tide of war began to turn against the Axis Powers by 1943. The United States, leveraging its vast industrial capacity, began to rebuild and expand its military forces. The Battle of Midway in June 1942 marked a significant turning point, as the U.S. Navy inflicted a decisive defeat on the Japanese fleet, halting Japan's advance in the Pacific.

The Allied powers, now fully mobilized, launched a series of counter offensives, gradually reclaiming territory from the Japanese. The island-hopping campaign in the Pacific, coupled with the relentless bombing of Japanese cities, weakened Japan's ability to sustain the war effort.

# CHAPTER SEVEN

# Japan's Anti-Western Psyche: A Story of Historical Grievances and Strategic Alignments

The Roots of Resentment

In the mid-19$^{th}$ century, Japan was forced to sign a series of unequal treaties by Western powers. This humiliating chapter began when Commodore Matthew Perry arrived in Edo Bay in 1853 with his intimidating "Black Ships." Under the threat of force, Japan opened its ports to American trade and, soon after, to other Western nations. These treaties imposed extraterritorial rights for Westerners and established tariff controls that heavily disadvantaged Japan. The national humiliation from these treaties fostered deep resentment and a sense of injustice.

As Japan modernized, its citizens and leaders perceived pervasive racial discrimination from Western powers. The U.S. Immigration Act of 1924, which effectively banned Japanese immigration, was a stark example. Such policies fueled a sense of racial injustice and reinforced Japan's desire to assert itself as an equal or superior power on the global stage.

Japan's proposal for a racial equality clause at the Paris Peace Conference of 1919 was another critical moment. Despite its contributions to World War I on the side of the Allies, Japan's proposal was rejected, primarily due to opposition from the United States and the British Empire. This diplomatic slight reinforced the perception that the Western powers did not regard Japan as an equal and were intent on maintaining racial hierarchies in international relations.

Economic Sanctions and Diplomatic Isolation

Japan's aggressive expansion in China and Southeast Asia led to economic sanctions and trade embargoes from the United States and other Western powers. The most significant of these was the U.S. oil embargo of 1941, which severely restricted Japan's access to crucial resources. These sanctions aimed to curb Japan's military ambitions but also deepened its economic hardships, further fueling anti-Western sentiment among Japanese leaders and the public.

Japan felt encircled by hostile Western powers determined to thwart its ambitions. This sense of encirclement was exacerbated by alliances such as the Anglo-American cooperation and various defense pacts among Western colonial powers in Asia. Japan viewed these alliances as efforts to contain its growth and influence, fostering further resentment and defiance.

Propaganda and Ideological Campaigns

The Japanese government and military propagated anti-Western sentiments through extensive use of propaganda. State-controlled media portrayed the West as decadent, morally corrupt, and oppressive, contrasting it with the purity and superiority of Japanese culture and values. This propaganda emphasized the narrative of Japan as the liberator of Asia from Western colonial rule.

The revival of Bushido, the way of the warrior, was integrated into the military and educational systems, reinforcing anti-Western attitudes. Bushido emphasized loyalty, honour, and self-sacrifice, fostering a militaristic spirit among the Japanese populace. This ideology supported the view that Japan had a divine mission to lead and protect Asia from Western exploitation.

Strategic and Political Calculations

Aligning with the Axis powers was seen as a strategic move to gain independence from Western dominance. By joining Germany and Italy, Japan hoped to break free from the constraints imposed by Western colonial and economic systems, establishing itself as a sovereign power capable of dictating its terms in international affairs.

The alliance with the Axis powers promised economic and military benefits that Japan could not obtain from the West. Germany's initial military successes in Europe demonstrated the potential of this alliance to achieve significant geopolitical gains. Japan aimed to capitalize on these successes to secure vital resources and strategic territories without Western interference.

Legacy and Consequences

Anti-Western sentiment contributed to the harsh treatment of Western prisoners of war and civilians during Japan's military campaigns. The dehumanization of Westerners, driven by propaganda and ideological indoctrination, led to widespread atrocities, including the Bataan Death March and the abuse of Allied POWs in Japanese camps.

The deep-rooted anti-Western sentiment had long-term implications for Japan's post-war relations. During the Allied occupation of Japan, efforts were made to eradicate militarism and promote democratic values. While the occupation led to significant reforms, it also required addressing the lingering resentment and rebuilding trust between Japan and Western nations.

In the aftermath of World War II, Japan's geopolitical alignment shifted dramatically. The Cold War context and the threat of communism led to a strategic partnership between Japan and the United States. This alliance was solidified by the U.S.-Japan Security Treaty, transforming former adversaries into key allies and reshaping Japan's foreign policy orientation.

The Impact of Historical Grievances

Japan's anti-Western sentiment was a complex interplay of historical grievances, economic pressures, and ideological indoctrination. It played a crucial role in driving Japan toward the Axis powers and influenced its wartime conduct and post-war recovery. Understanding this sentiment provides critical insights into Japan's actions during World War II and its subsequent evolution as a nation.

The economic sanctions and embargoes imposed by the United States and its allies severely restricted Japan's access to crucial resources like oil, rubber, and metals. Aligning with the Axis powers provided Japan with a strategic pathway to seize resource-rich territories in Southeast Asia, including the Dutch East Indies (modern-day Indonesia), Malaya, and the Philippines.

By joining the Axis powers, Japan aimed to counterbalance the influence of the Western colonial powers in Asia. The Tripartite Pact, signed in 1940, established a military alliance with Germany and Italy, providing Japan with the political and military support needed to challenge Western dominance in the region.

Throughout the 1930s, Japan's actions in Asia, particularly its invasion of Manchuria in 1931 and its brutal war in China starting in 1937, isolated it diplomatically from the Western powers. The United States and its allies condemned Japan's aggression, leading to deteriorating relations and economic sanctions.

Japan's diplomatic efforts in the 1930s included non-aggression pacts and military cooperation with Axis powers. The Anti-Comintern Pact signed with Germany in 1936, and later joined by Italy, was directed against the Soviet Union but also symbolized a broader alignment against Western democracies.

The Calculations Behind the Alliance

The Axis alliance offered mutual strategic benefits. While Germany and Italy focused on their European campaigns, Japan's aggressive actions in Asia diverted Allied resources and attention. This coordination aimed to stretch the Allies' military capabilities across multiple fronts, creating opportunities for Axis victories in different theaters.

Given the hostile relations with the United States and the British Empire, Japan had limited viable alternatives for powerful allies.

The Soviet Union, despite being a potential partner, was viewed with suspicion due to ideological differences and historical conflicts. Japan's previous military confrontations with the Soviets, such as the Battles of Khalkhin Gol in 1939, further strained relations, making the Axis alliance a more pragmatic choice.

During the late 1930s and early 1940s, Germany's military successes in Europe and North Africa projected an image of strength and invincibility. Japan believed that aligning with a seemingly dominant Axis coalition would provide a better chance of achieving its imperial goals and securing a favourable position in the new world order envisioned by Axis leaders.

This intricate interplay of historical grievances, economic pressures, and ideological beliefs shaped Japan's anti-Western psyche, driving it to align with the Axis powers. This alignment had far-reaching consequences, influencing Japan's wartime behaviour, its post-war recovery, and its long-term geopolitical strategies. Understanding these factors provides a nuanced perspective on Japan's actions during this tumultuous period and its evolution in the aftermath.

# CHAPTER EIGHT

# The Treaty of Versailles: A Turning Point for Japan

After the conclusion of World War I, Japan, having aligned with the victorious Allied powers, anticipated that it would gain both recognition and territorial rewards. The Treaty of Versailles was supposed to mark a significant moment in Japan's ascent as a major global power. As part of the spoils, Japan gained control over former German territories in the Pacific and China, specifically the South Pacific Mandate and the German concessions in Shandong Province. These acquisitions expanded Japan's influence and provided valuable strategic and economic resources. However, the treaty also sowed seeds of dissatisfaction and resentment that would deeply influence Japan's future policies and national psyche.

During the Versailles Conference, Japan proposed a racial equality clause to be included in the League of Nations Covenant. This clause, if accepted, would affirm racial equality and non-discrimination, reflecting Japan's desire to be seen as an equal among Western powers. Despite receiving majority support from the conference delegates, the proposal was blocked, primarily due to opposition from the United States and the British Empire. These nations feared the implications such a clause would have on their immigration policies and colonial holdings. This rejection was not merely a diplomatic setback; it was a profound humiliation that left a lasting scar on Japan's national pride.

The immediate economic benefits of Japan's territorial gains were significant. The new territories offered opportunities for resource extraction and strategic military positioning. However, these gains came at a time of global economic instability. The Great Depression, which began in the late 1920s, severely impacted Japan's economy, leading to widespread hardship. The economic challenges exacerbated existing political instability and increased support for militaristic and expansionist policies among the Japanese populace and leadership.

The dissatisfaction with the international order established by the Treaty of Versailles fueled a shift in Japanese foreign policy. Japan's leaders, feeling snubbed by the rejection of the racial equality proposal and disillusioned by the limitations imposed by Western powers, concluded that Japan needed to strengthen its military capabilities. This period saw a significant increase in military influence over Japanese politics and society, as the military was seen as the vehicle through which Japan could secure its interests and achieve its goals.

Nationalistic and militaristic ideologies gained traction, advocating for Japanese expansionism as a means to secure resources, territory, and recognition as a great power. The sense of injustice and the desire to overturn the Western-dominated international order contributed to Japan's aggressive foreign policy in the following decades. The invasion of Manchuria in 1931 and the establishment of the puppet state of Manchukuo were early signs of Japan's expansionist ambitions, driven by the belief that Japan was destined to lead Asia and resist Western domination.

The events surrounding the Treaty of Versailles also strained Japan's relations with Western powers, particularly the United States and Britain. The perception of racial discrimination and unequal treatment deepened mistrust and led to Japan's increasing alienation from the Western-dominated international system. This alienation set Japan on a path toward forging new alliances and finding strategic partners who shared its dissatisfaction with the status quo.

Japan's growing dissatisfaction with the international order culminated in the formation of the Tripartite Pact with Germany and Italy in 1940. This alliance was part of Japan's strategy to counterbalance Western power and secure its expansionist ambitions in Asia and the Pacific. The pact symbolized Japan's shift away from cooperation with Western powers and towards a more aggressive and independent foreign policy.

The sense of grievance and desire for revisionism that emerged from the Treaty of Versailles played a crucial role in shaping Japan's trajectory towards World War II. Japan's aggressive actions in Asia, including the invasion of China in 1937 and the attack on Pearl Harbor in 1941, were driven by the ambition to establish a Greater East Asia Co-Prosperity Sphere and challenge Western dominance. These actions ultimately led to Japan's involvement in a global conflict that would have devastating consequences.

The legacy of the Treaty of Versailles continued to influence the post-World War II international order. After Japan's defeat in 1945, the Allied occupation led to significant political, economic, and social reforms. These reforms aimed to address some of the issues that had contributed to the failures of the Versailles system, including the establishment of the United Nations, which sought to promote inclusive and equitable international agreements.

In conclusion, the Treaty of Versailles had a profound impact on Japan, influencing its foreign policy, national identity, and trajectory towards militarism and expansionism. The rejection of the racial equality proposal, combined with the broader economic and strategic implications of the treaty, fueled a sense of injustice and resentment that shaped Japan's actions in the interwar period and beyond. The treaty's legacy serves as a reminder of the importance of inclusive and equitable international agreements in promoting lasting peace and stability.

Delegates signed the Treaty of Versailles in the former palace's famous Hall of Mirrors, ending World War I.(National Geography)

# CHAPTER NINE

# The Race for the Atom Bomb: A Tale of Ambition, Science, and War

Prologue: The Dawn of Nuclear Science

In the early 20th century, the world of science was buzzing with revolutionary discoveries. Among these was the groundbreaking work on the atom, the smallest unit of matter, which held secrets that could change the course of history. Physicists like Ernest Rutherford and Niels Bohr were unravelling the mysteries of atomic structure, setting the stage for an extraordinary and dangerous race: the development of the atomic bomb.

In 1938, in a laboratory in Berlin, German physicists Otto Hahn and Fritz Strassmann made a startling discovery. While bombarding uranium with neutrons, they observed that the uranium nucleus had split into lighter elements, releasing a significant amount of energy. This process, known as nuclear fission, was later explained by Lise Meitner and Otto Frisch, who fled Nazi Germany and reported their findings to the international scientific community.

News of this discovery spread rapidly. The potential for a bomb of unprecedented power became a real possibility. Scientists around the world, including those who had fled Europe to escape the growing threat of Nazi Germany, realized the implications. Among them were Albert Einstein and Leo Szilard, who were deeply concerned about the possibility of Nazi Germany developing such a weapon.

In 1939, as tensions in Europe were escalating towards war, Leo Szilard and fellow physicist Eugene Wigner convinced Albert Einstein to write a letter to President Franklin D. Roosevelt. In this letter, Einstein warned that Germany might be working on an atomic bomb and urged the United States to begin similar research. This letter was delivered to Roosevelt, who, after initial scepticism, established the Advisory Committee on Uranium, marking the beginning of the U.S. atomic bomb project.

By 1942, the United States had entered World War II, and the need for an atomic bomb became urgent. The Manhattan Project was born, a secret and massive effort to build the world's first nuclear weapon. Directed by General Leslie Groves and scientific leader J. Robert Oppenheimer, the project brought together some of the greatest minds in physics, chemistry, and engineering.

The project was spread across multiple sites in the United States, with the primary research and design center at Los Alamos, New Mexico. Scientists like Enrico Fermi, Richard Feynman, and Niels Bohr worked tirelessly, driven by both scientific curiosity and the pressing need to defeat the Axis powers.

While the Manhattan Project was the most well-known and well-funded effort, other nations were also making strides in nuclear research. In Germany, under the guidance of physicists such as Werner Heisenberg, efforts were made to develop a bomb. However, various challenges, including resource allocation, bureaucratic inefficiencies, and strategic bombings by the Allies, hindered their progress.

In Britain, the Tube Alloys project was established to pursue atomic research. This project later merged with the Manhattan Project, bringing British scientists like James Chadwick and Klaus Fuchs into the fold. Unbeknownst to many, Fuchs was a Soviet spy who passed crucial information to the Soviet Union, helping them accelerate their own atomic program.

The Soviet Union, initially behind in the nuclear race, ramped up their efforts under the leadership of Igor Kurchatov. Using intelligence gathered by spies like Fuchs and Theodore Hall, the Soviets made significant strides in their own bomb development.

After years of intense research and development, the Manhattan Project reached a critical point. On July 16, 1945, in the New Mexico desert, the first atomic bomb, codenamed "Trinity," was tested. The explosion was more powerful than anyone had anticipated, lighting up the sky with a blinding flash and generating a mushroom cloud that rose miles into the air. The success of the Trinity test meant that the United States now possessed a weapon of unimaginable destructive power.

With the successful test of the atomic bomb, the United States faced a fateful decision. President Harry S. Truman, after consultations with his military and scientific advisors, decided to use the bomb to hasten the end of the war with Japan. On August 6, 1945, the B-29 bomber Enola Gay dropped the first atomic bomb, codenamed "Little Boy," on the city of Hiroshima. The devastation was immediate and catastrophic, killing tens of thousands of people instantly and leveling the city.

Three days later, on August 9, a second bomb, codenamed "Fat Man," was dropped on Nagasaki. The destruction was equally devastating. Faced with the overwhelming power of the atomic bombs and the Soviet Union's declaration of war, Japan surrendered on August 15, 1945, bringing World War II to an end.

In the aftermath of World War II, the Soviet Union accelerated its atomic bomb program, determined not to be left behind in the nuclear arms race. Using information obtained from espionage and their own scientific research, the Soviets successfully tested their first atomic bomb on August 29, 1949. The explosion, known as "First Lightning," marked the beginning of the nuclear arms race between the United States and the Soviet Union, a central element of the Cold War.

The United States and the Soviet Union were not the only countries to develop nuclear weapons. Britain, which had contributed to the Manhattan Project, continued its own research after the war. In 1952, Britain successfully tested its first atomic bomb, becoming the third nuclear power.

France, driven by a desire to maintain its independence and strategic autonomy, also pursued nuclear weapons. Under the leadership of President Charles de Gaulle, France conducted its first successful nuclear test in 1960, solidifying its status as a nuclear power.

The development of atomic bombs had profound implications for international relations and global security. The immense destructive power of these weapons fundamentally altered the nature of warfare and diplomacy. The Cold War was characterized by a tense standoff between the United States and the Soviet Union, each armed with enough nuclear weapons to destroy the other many times over. This balance of terror, known as Mutually Assured Destruction (MAD), helped prevent direct conflict between the superpowers but also led to numerous proxy wars and a constant state of global tension.

The existence of nuclear weapons also prompted efforts to control their spread. The Nuclear Non-Proliferation Treaty (NPT), signed in 1968, aimed to prevent the proliferation of nuclear weapons and promote disarmament. Despite these efforts, several other countries, including China, India, and Pakistan, developed nuclear capabilities, further complicating global security dynamics.

The development and use of atomic bombs raised profound ethical questions. The bombings of Hiroshima and Nagasaki, while hastening the end of World War II, resulted in immense human suffering and loss of life. The decision to use such a weapon was and remains a deeply controversial topic, with debates about the necessity and morality of using nuclear weapons continuing to this day.

Scientists who worked on the Manhattan Project, including J. Robert Oppenheimer, grappled with the ethical implications of their work. Oppenheimer famously quoted the Bhagavad Gita, saying, "Now I am become Death, the destroyer of worlds," reflecting his inner turmoil over the destructive power he had helped unleash.

The race to develop the atomic bomb was a story of scientific achievement, strategic necessity, and moral complexity. It brought together some of the brightest minds of the 20th century, who, driven by the exigencies of war, unlocked the secrets of the atom and changed the course of history.

The legacy of the atomic bomb is still felt today. The threat of nuclear warfare continues to loom over the world, prompting efforts towards disarmament and the peaceful use of nuclear technology. The story of the atom bomb serves as a powerful reminder of the potential for both human ingenuity and destructiveness, and the ongoing need to manage this delicate balance responsibly.

# CHAPTER TEN

# The Potsdam Conference: A Turning Point in World War II

The Potsdam Conference: A Turning Point in World War II

In the heat of summer, in July 1945, leaders of the Allied powers converged in the quiet suburb of Potsdam, near Berlin. This gathering, known as the Potsdam Conference, marked a crucial moment in the final stages of World War II. The conference was attended by Joseph Stalin, leader of the Soviet Union; Winston Churchill, soon to be replaced by Clement Attlee, Prime Minister of the United Kingdom; and Harry S. Truman, the newly sworn-in President of the United States. Each of these men carried the weight of their nations' hopes and the responsibility of shaping the post-war world.

The grand Cecilienhof Palace, with its Tudor-style architecture, served as the backdrop for the conference. Despite the serene setting, the atmosphere was charged with urgency and tension. The Allies had achieved victory in Europe, but the war in the Pacific raged on. The conference aimed to address various geopolitical issues, but a significant focus was on how to bring about Japan's unconditional surrender.

The Leaders and Their Agendas

President Truman arrived at Potsdam with a steely determination. He had recently succeeded Franklin D. Roosevelt and was eager to assert his leadership on the global stage. Truman was acutely aware of the secret weapon the United States possessed—the atomic bomb, which had just been successfully tested in New Mexico. This new weapon was a key part of his strategy to force Japan to surrender.

Stalin, ever the shrewd tactician, sought to expand Soviet influence in Eastern Europe and Asia. He was committed to securing Soviet interests and ensuring that the USSR emerged from the war as a dominant global power. Stalin's willingness to join the war against Japan, as agreed at the Yalta Conference earlier that year, was a crucial factor in the discussions.

Churchill, an iconic wartime leader, attended the conference with a sense of continuity and experience. However, midway through the conference, he was replaced by Clement Attlee after losing the general election. Attlee, though less charismatic, brought a new perspective to the table, focusing on post-war recovery and reconstruction.

The Potsdam Declaration

The Potsdam Conference led to the issuance of the Potsdam Declaration on July 26, 1945. This declaration outlined the terms of surrender for Japan, offering them a final chance to avoid total destruction. The terms were stern but clear: Japan must surrender unconditionally, or face "prompt and utter destruction." The declaration also promised that Japan would not be enslaved or destroyed as a nation, and that its people would be allowed to live in peace once a responsible government was established.

However, the declaration was notable for what it did not mention—the atomic bomb. Truman and his advisors decided to keep the bomb a secret, preferring to use it as a last resort if Japan did not surrender. This omission added to the declaration's ominous tone, leaving Japan uncertain about the exact nature of the threat they faced.

Japan's Response

Japan's leadership, particularly the military factions, was divided on how to respond to the Potsdam Declaration. Some advocated for continuing the fight, hoping for better surrender terms or for Soviet mediation. Others, recognizing the dire situation, argued for surrender. The Japanese government ultimately chose to ignore the declaration publicly, viewing it as a threat that lacked the force to compel immediate action.

The Role of the Soviet Union

The Potsdam Conference also solidified the Soviet Union's commitment to enter the war against Japan. Stalin agreed to launch an attack on Japanese forces in Manchuria by mid-August, aligning with the timeline set by the Allies. This agreement was a critical strategic move that would put additional pressure on Japan from the north, further isolating the island nation and stretching its already thin resources.

The Isolation of Japan

The decisions made at Potsdam effectively isolated Japan both militarily and diplomatically. The Allied powers were united in their demand for unconditional surrender, and the Soviet Union's entry into the war meant that Japan was now facing a multi-front battle it could not hope to win. The combination of the Potsdam Declaration and the looming Soviet invasion left Japan with dwindling options and an increasingly bleak outlook.

The Aftermath

On August 6, 1945, less than two weeks after the Potsdam Declaration was issued, the United States dropped the atomic bomb on Hiroshima. Three days later, on August 9, another bomb was dropped on Nagasaki. The devastation was unimaginable, and the combined pressure of the atomic bombings and the Soviet invasion of Manchuria finally broke the Japanese will to continue fighting.

On August 15, 1945, Emperor Hirohito announced Japan's surrender, bringing an end to World War II. The Potsdam Conference, with its strategic decisions and the issuance of the Potsdam Declaration, had played a pivotal role in isolating Japan and setting the stage for its eventual surrender.

The Potsdam Conference is remembered as a critical juncture in the closing chapter of World War II. The decisions made there not only contributed to the end of the war but also shaped the geopolitical landscape of the post-war world. The conference underscored the importance of Allied unity and demonstrated the devastating power of nuclear weapons. It also highlighted the complex interplay of military strategy and diplomatic negotiations in achieving peace.

The story of the Potsdam Conference is a testament to the high-stakes diplomacy that can define the course of history. It reminds us of the immense responsibilities borne by leaders in times of global crisis and the profound impact of their decisions on the fate of nations.

The "Big Three": Attlee, Truman, Stalin ( Wikipedia)

# CHAPTER ELEVEN

# Possible Hidden Reasons Behind Bombing Nagasaki Just Three Days After Hiroshima

Demonstrating Resolve and Power

Demonstration of Multiple Capabilities: By bombing Nagasaki just three days after Hiroshima, the United States demonstrated its capability to produce and deploy multiple atomic bombs in quick succession. This was a clear signal to both Japan and the rest of the world, particularly the Soviet Union, of the formidable power and technological prowess of the United States. It underscored that Hiroshima was not an isolated event but part of a sustained capacity for nuclear warfare.

Psychological Impact: The rapid succession of the bombings was intended to maximize the psychological shock and awe on the Japanese leadership. The intent was to convey that the United States could continue to deliver such devastating blows indefinitely, thereby undermining any hope Japan might have had for a prolonged resistance or negotiation on more favorable terms.

Political and Diplomatic Considerations

Influence on Soviet Union: At the Potsdam Conference, there were already emerging tensions between the United States and the

Soviet Union. The bombings served as a geopolitical message to the Soviets, showcasing the United States' new military superiority and potentially influencing post-war negotiations and the balance of power in the emerging Cold War context. The rapidity of the second bombing underscored the urgency and the scale of the new threat.

Prompting Japanese Surrender: There was a strategic calculation that a second bombing would hasten Japan's decision to surrender. After the bombing of Hiroshima, there was still debate within the Japanese government about whether to surrender or continue fighting. The bombing of Nagasaki was intended to break the will of the Japanese leadership and force a swift conclusion to the war, preventing further loss of life and resources on both sides.

Military and Strategic Rationales

Testing Different Bomb Designs: The bombs dropped on Hiroshima and Nagasaki were of different designs: "Little Boy" (a uranium-based bomb) and "Fat Man" (a plutonium-based bomb). The bombing of Nagasaki provided an opportunity to test the effectiveness of the plutonium bomb in actual combat conditions. This was not just about evaluating the bomb's destructive capacity but also understanding the logistical and operational aspects of deploying different types of nuclear weapons.

Evaluating Impact on Different Terrains: Hiroshima and Nagasaki had different geographical and structural characteristics. By bombing two distinct cities, the U.S. could assess the bomb's impact on varying urban environments, providing valuable data for future strategic planning. Nagasaki's hilly terrain offered a contrast to the relatively flat terrain of Hiroshima, allowing for a comparative analysis of the bomb's effects.

Tactical Timing

Maintaining Pressure: The three-day interval between the bombings was tactically designed to maintain continuous pressure on the Japanese government. Any longer delay might have allowed Japan to better assess the situation, potentially diminishing the psychological impact and giving the Japanese military time to regroup or counteract. The swift follow-up bombing ensured that the momentum of shock and devastation was sustained.

Avoiding Soviet Influence in Japan's Surrender: The Soviet Union declared war on Japan on August 8, 1945, and began its invasion of Japanese-held territories in Manchuria. By hastening Japan's surrender through a second bombing, the United States aimed to end the war before the Soviets could establish a significant presence in Japan. This was crucial for shaping the post-war order in East Asia and limiting Soviet influence in the region.

Scientific and Ethical Considerations

Data Collection and Analysis: Beyond immediate military objectives, the bombings provided scientists with real-world data on the effects of nuclear explosions on human populations, buildings, and the environment. This data was considered essential for understanding the full implications of nuclear warfare and for developing future military strategies and policies. However, this rationale raises profound ethical questions about the use of human populations as subjects for such experiments.

Moral Justification and Momentum: Once the decision to use atomic bombs had been made and the first bomb dropped, there was likely a momentum to continue with the planned operations. The moral and ethical justifications for using the bomb—ending the war swiftly, saving lives in the long run—had already been established. This momentum, combined with the lack of immediate Japanese surrender after Hiroshima, likely contributed to the decision to proceed with the Nagasaki bombing.

The decision to bomb Nagasaki just three days after Hiroshima was influenced by a complex interplay of military strategy, political considerations, psychological warfare, and scientific experimentation. While the primary stated goal was to hasten Japan's surrender and end World War II, there were also significant underlying motives related to demonstrating power, influencing global geopolitics, and gathering data on nuclear weapons. These factors combined to create a situation where the devastating bombing of Nagasaki became a pivotal, albeit controversial, moment in history.

# CHAPTER TWELVE

# The Blunders of Attacking Pearl Harbor

On a tranquil Sunday morning, December 7, 1941, the sun rose over the Hawaiian island of Oahu, casting a serene light over the waters of Pearl Harbor. The American naval base lay quiet, with ships anchored in neat rows and sailors beginning their day with the routine of a peaceful peacetime Sunday. But beneath this veneer of calm, a storm was brewing—a storm that would forever alter the course of World War II and seal the fate of the Empire of Japan.

High above the Pacific Ocean, a fleet of Japanese aircraft carriers cut through the waves, carrying a lethal cargo of bombers, fighters, and torpedo planes. The Japanese Imperial Navy had embarked on a bold and audacious mission, one that they believed would cripple the United States Navy and give Japan the upper hand in its quest for dominance in the Pacific. This mission, meticulously planned and rehearsed, was the surprise attack on Pearl Harbor.

Admiral Isoroku Yamamoto, the mastermind behind the attack, was acutely aware of the risks involved. He had studied in the United States and understood the industrial might and resolve of the American people. Yet, driven by a combination of strategic necessity and nationalistic fervor, he pressed forward with the plan. Yamamoto believed that a decisive blow at Pearl Harbor would demoralize the United States and delay its ability to project power across the Pacific.

The decision to attack Pearl Harbor was influenced by several key factors, each playing a crucial role in shaping Japan's strategy.

Resource Scarcity and Economic Sanctions :By the late 1930s, Japan's aggressive expansion in Asia had led to significant territorial gains, but it had also resulted in economic and political isolation. Japan relied heavily on imports for critical resources such as oil, steel, and rubber, which were essential for its military and industrial operations. In response to Japan's invasion of China and its occupation of French Indochina, the United States, along with other Western powers, imposed stringent economic sanctions and trade embargoes.

The most crippling of these was the U.S. oil embargo, which threatened to strangle Japan's war machine. Faced with the prospect of running out of vital resources within months, Japan saw its survival and continued expansion as dependent on securing access to the natural resources of Southeast Asia, particularly the oil-rich Dutch East Indies (modern-day Indonesia).

Strategic Military Objectives:Japan's military leadership recognized that to secure and maintain control over Southeast Asia, they needed to neutralize the United States Pacific Fleet, which was stationed at Pearl Harbor. The fleet represented the most significant obstacle to Japan's southward expansion. By incapacitating the U.S. Navy, Japan hoped to buy time to consolidate its territorial gains and build a formidable defensive perimeter stretching across the Pacific.

Psychological and Diplomatic Considerations:Japan also sought to deliver a psychological blow that would deter the United States from entering the war in the Pacific. Japanese leaders believed that a devastating surprise attack would shock and demoralize the American public, forcing the U.S. government to negotiate peace on terms favourable to Japan. This belief was partly based on the perception that American society, unlike the militarized and disciplined Japanese, was not prepared for a prolonged and brutal conflict.

Misjudgment of American Resolve:One of the most significant blunders of the Pearl Harbor attack was the gross underestimation of American resolve and capability. Japanese military leaders, including Admiral Yamamoto, believed that a surprise attack would shatter American morale and force the United States into a defensive posture, buying Japan time to consolidate its gains in Southeast Asia.

However, the attack had the opposite effect. The sight of burning ships and the loss of thousands of American lives ignited a fierce determination in the American public and leadership. President Franklin D. Roosevelt's address to Congress on December 8, famously declaring the date as "a date which will live in infamy," rallied the nation. The United States declared war on Japan, and a sleeping giant was awakened.

The attack on Pearl Harbor unified the American people in a way that few events could. Recruitment offices were flooded with volunteers eager to join the fight, and the nation's industrial might was mobilized to produce the weapons and supplies needed for a global war. The Japanese had miscalculated the resilience and resourcefulness of their adversary, turning what they hoped would be a crippling blow into a galvanizing call to arms.

The Failure to Destroy Key Targets : Another critical blunder of the Pearl Harbor attack was the failure to target and destroy key military assets. While the attack inflicted significant damage on the battleships and killed over 2,400 Americans, it missed several crucial targets that would have had a far more devastating impact on the United States' ability to wage war in the Pacific.

The Japanese attackers failed to destroy the American aircraft carriers, which were not present in the harbour at the time of the attack. These carriers, including the USS Enterprise, USS Lexington, and USS Saratoga, would later play pivotal roles in the Pacific Theater, contributing to key victories such as the Battle of Midway.

Additionally, the attack did not target the extensive fuel storage facilities and repair docks at Pearl Harbor. These facilities were vital for the American Navy's operational capabilities in the Pacific.

Had the Japanese destroyed the fuel reserves, the U.S. fleet would have been severely hampered in its ability to conduct long-range operations. The repair docks, left largely intact, allowed damaged ships to be quickly restored to service, ensuring that the Pacific Fleet could recover and strike back.

Strategic Overreach and the Broadening of the War : The attack on Pearl Harbor represented a strategic overreach by Japan, a nation that was already stretched thin by its ongoing conflicts in China and its ambitions in Southeast Asia. By attacking the United States, Japan expanded the scope of its war effort dramatically, taking on an adversary with far greater industrial capacity and resources.

The United States, now fully committed to the war, leveraged its vast industrial base to outproduce and outmanoeuvre Japan. The American strategy of "island hopping," combined with relentless submarine warfare that targeted Japanese supply lines, gradually strangled Japan's ability to sustain its war effort. The initial gains made by Japan in the early months of the war were slowly reversed, and the Allies began their inexorable advance towards the Japanese home islands.

The Underestimation of Long-Term Consequences

In their eagerness to strike a decisive blow, Japanese planners failed to fully consider the long-term consequences of their actions. The attack on Pearl Harbor not only provoked the United States into the war but also solidified the alliance between the United States, the United Kingdom, and the Soviet Union. This coalition of major powers brought immense pressure to bear on the Axis, ultimately leading to the defeat of Japan and its allies.

Moreover, the attack altered the geopolitical landscape in ways that Japanese leaders had not anticipated. The United States emerged from World War II as a dominant global power, with a permanent military presence in the Pacific and a significant role in shaping the post-war international order. Japan, on the other hand, faced occupation, demilitarization, and the challenge of rebuilding a devastated nation.

Yamamoto's Foreboding Realisation

Admiral Yamamoto, despite being the architect of the attack, harboured deep reservations about its long-term implications. Legend has it that, upon learning of the successful attack, he remarked, "I fear all we have done is to awaken a sleeping giant and fill him with a terrible resolve." Whether or not these words were actually spoken, they captured the essence of Yamamoto's understanding of the broader strategic picture.

Yamamoto knew that Japan's industrial capacity was no match for that of the United States and that a protracted war would favour the Americans. His fears were realized as the United States rapidly mobilized, outproduced, and outmanoeuvred Japan in the ensuing conflict.

The Lasting Impact of Strategic Miscalculations

The attack on Pearl Harbor, while initially a tactical success, was a strategic blunder that set the stage for Japan's eventual defeat. The underestimation of American resolve, the failure to destroy key military assets, the strategic overreach, and the miscalculation of long-term consequences all contributed to the unraveling of Japan's war effort.

The legacy of Pearl Harbor is a powerful reminder of the complexities of war and the importance of strategic foresight. It underscores the dangers of underestimating an opponent and the profound impact that a single decision can have on the course of history.

As the sun set on December 7, 1941, the fires at Pearl Harbor still smouldered, and the United States prepared to enter the most devastating conflict in human history. The blunders of attacking Pearl Harbor became evident in the years that followed, as the tide of war turned against Japan, leading to the inevitable reckoning that would come with the bombings of Hiroshima and Nagasaki.

In the end, the attack on Pearl Harbor serves as a sombre lesson in the annals of military history—a lesson about the far-reaching consequences of strategic miscalculations and the indomitable spirit of a nation awakened by tragedy.

Attack on Pearl Harbor

# CHAPTER THIRTEEN

# Prelude to the Bomb: The Road to Hiroshima and Nagasaki

Prelude to the Bomb: The Road to Hiroshima and Nagasaki

The Dawn of the Nuclear Age

The story of the atomic bomb's development and its eventual use on Hiroshima and Nagasaki begins with the burgeoning field of nuclear physics in the early 20th century. Scientists around the world were unravelling the mysteries of the atom, leading to groundbreaking discoveries that would forever change the course of history.

Early Discoveries: In 1898, Marie and Pierre Curie discovered radioactivity, a phenomenon that piqued the interest of physicists. By 1938, German scientists Otto Hahn and Fritz Strassmann, along with Lise Meitner and Otto Frisch, discovered nuclear fission, the process by which an atomic nucleus splits into two smaller nuclei, releasing a massive amount of energy.

Global Implications: The potential military applications of nuclear fission became apparent quickly. Scientists realized that harnessing this energy could lead to the creation of extraordinarily powerful weapons. The outbreak of World War II accelerated these considerations, as nations sought any possible advantage.

The Manhattan Project

Scientific Exodus and Einstein's Letter: The rise of Adolf Hitler and the Nazi regime in Germany led many prominent scientists, particularly those of Jewish descent, to flee Europe. Among them were physicists like Albert Einstein and Leo Szilard, who were deeply concerned about the possibility of Nazi Germany developing nuclear weapons. In 1939, Einstein and Szilard wrote a letter to U.S. President Franklin D. Roosevelt, warning him of this potential threat and urging the U.S. to pursue its own research into nuclear weapons.

Formation of the Manhattan Project: In response, Roosevelt authorized preliminary research, which soon evolved into the Manhattan Project—a massive, top-secret endeavour to develop atomic bombs. The project brought together some of the greatest scientific minds, including J. Robert Oppenheimer, Enrico Fermi, and Niels Bohr. With facilities spread across the United States, the most notable being Los Alamos in New Mexico, the project aimed to achieve a working atomic bomb before the Axis powers.

Scientific Breakthroughs: The Manhattan Project faced numerous technical challenges, from producing sufficient quantities of fissile material (uranium-235 and plutonium-239) to designing a bomb that could effectively trigger a nuclear chain reaction. Through relentless effort and ingenuity, these obstacles were overcome, leading to the first successful test of an atomic bomb on July 16, 1945, at the Trinity site in New Mexico.

The Geopolitical Context

World War II Escalates: As the Manhattan Project progressed, the war raged on multiple fronts. The Allies, comprising the United States, the United Kingdom, the Soviet Union, and others, fought fiercely against the Axis powers of Germany, Italy, and Japan. By mid-1945, Germany had been defeated, but the war in the Pacific continued with brutal intensity.

Japanese Expansion and Aggression: Japan had been pursuing a policy of aggressive expansion throughout Asia and the Pacific since the early 1930s. The invasion of Manchuria in 1931, the Second Sino-Japanese War in 1937, and the surprise attack on Pearl

Harbor in 1941 highlighted Japan's ambitions and willingness to use military force to achieve its goals. The attack on Pearl Harbor brought the United States into the war, drastically altering the balance of power in the Pacific.

American Blockade and Strategic Bombing: By 1944, the United States had established naval and air superiority in the Pacific, implementing a blockade that severely restricted Japan's ability to import essential resources. Strategic bombing raids devastated Japanese cities, infrastructure, and industry, yet Japan continued to resist fiercely, exemplified by the battles of Iwo Jima and Okinawa, where Allied forces faced intense and costly resistance.

The Decision to Use the Bomb

Potsdam Conference: In July 1945, Allied leaders met at the Potsdam Conference to discuss the post-war order and issue terms of surrender for Japan. The Potsdam Declaration called for Japan's unconditional surrender, warning of "prompt and utter destruction" if it failed to comply. Japan's government, however, was divided on the issue, with hardliners advocating for continued resistance.

Weighing the Options: President Harry S. Truman, who had succeeded Roosevelt in April 1945, faced a difficult decision. The prospect of a costly invasion of the Japanese mainland, which could result in hundreds of thousands of Allied and Japanese casualties, weighed heavily. The successful Trinity test had demonstrated the destructive power of the atomic bomb, presenting Truman with a potential means to force Japan's surrender without a protracted invasion.

Ethical and Strategic Considerations: The decision to use the bomb was not taken lightly. Truman and his advisors considered various factors, including the potential to save lives by avoiding an invasion, the desire to swiftly end the war, and the opportunity to demonstrate the bomb's power to the world, particularly the Soviet Union, with whom post-war tensions were already emerging.

Hiroshima and Nagasaki

Hiroshima: On August 6, 1945, the B-29 bomber Enola Gay dropped the atomic bomb "Little Boy" on the city of Hiroshima. The explosion unleashed unprecedented destruction, instantly killing tens of thousands and devastating the city. The shockwaves of the blast and the ensuing radiation caused further casualties, eventually claiming the lives of approximately 140,000 people by the end of the year.

Nagasaki: Despite the devastation of Hiroshima, the Japanese government did not immediately surrender. On August 9, 1945, a second atomic bomb, "Fat Man," was dropped on Nagasaki. The hilly terrain of Nagasaki limited the bomb's destructive radius compared to Hiroshima, but it still caused massive destruction and loss of life, with an estimated 70,000 deaths by the end of 1945.

The Aftermath and Legacy

Japan's Surrender: The combined shock of the atomic bombings and the Soviet Union's declaration of war on Japan on August 8, 1945, led to Japan's surrender. On August 15, Emperor Hirohito announced Japan's acceptance of the Potsdam Declaration, and the formal surrender was signed on September 2, 1945, aboard the USS Missouri in Tokyo Bay, officially ending World War II.

Human Cost and Ethical Debates: The bombings of Hiroshima and Nagasaki resulted in immense human suffering, with immediate and long-term effects of radiation causing deaths and chronic health issues for survivors (hibakusha). The ethical implications of using such devastating weapons on civilian populations have been debated ever since, raising questions about the morality of nuclear warfare and the responsibilities of those who wield such power.

Geopolitical Impact: The use of atomic bombs significantly influenced post-war geopolitics. The bombings demonstrated the United States' technological and military superiority, shaping the early dynamics of the Cold War. The Soviet Union accelerated its own nuclear weapons program, leading to an arms race that defined much of the 20th century.

Nuclear Proliferation and Disarmament: The legacy of Hiroshima and Nagasaki has had a profound impact on global efforts to control nuclear weapons. The bombings underscored the catastrophic potential of nuclear warfare, leading to international treaties aimed at preventing proliferation and promoting disarmament, such as the Treaty on the Non-Proliferation of Nuclear Weapons (NPT) and various arms control agreements.

The prelude to the atomic bombings of Hiroshima and Nagasaki is a complex narrative of scientific discovery, wartime strategy, and profound ethical considerations. It encompasses the relentless pursuit of knowledge, the horrors of global conflict, and the quest for power that defined an era. The bombings not only brought an end to World War II but also ushered in the nuclear age, forever altering the course of human history and leaving a legacy that continues to shape our world today.

# CHAPTER FOURTEEN

# Hiroshima vs. Nagasaki: A Comprehensive Comparative Study

The Fateful Decision

In the summer of 1945, the Allied forces were closing in on victory in the Pacific Theater. The relentless battles on islands like Iwo Jima and Okinawa had demonstrated the fierce resistance of Japanese forces and the high cost of a potential invasion of the Japanese mainland. President Harry S. Truman, newly sworn in after the death of Franklin D. Roosevelt, faced an agonizing decision. On his desk was the most powerful weapon ever created by mankind: the atomic bomb.

The decision to use the bomb was influenced by several factors, including the desire to end the war swiftly, to minimize further Allied casualties, and to demonstrate the overwhelming power of the United States to the rest of the world, particularly the Soviet Union. The target selection process began in earnest, with military and scientific advisors presenting potential sites.

The Choice of Targets

In April 1945, the Target Committee, composed of military leaders and scientists, convened to discuss suitable targets for the atomic bomb. The committee considered various cities for their military and industrial significance, as well as their psychological impact on Japan.

Hiroshima, a city of approximately 350,000 people, was a major military command center and supply depot. Its relatively untouched state would allow for an accurate assessment of the bomb's destructive power. Nagasaki, an important industrial city with shipyards, steelworks, and armament factories, was also identified as a potential target. Kokura and Kyoto were considered but eventually removed from the list, Kyoto for its cultural significance and Kokura due to weather conditions on the day of the bombing.

The final decision was to bomb Hiroshima first, with Kokura as the secondary target and Nagasaki as the tertiary. The plan was set into motion with a grim determination to bring the war to a conclusive end.

Hiroshima Before the Bomb

Hiroshima was a bustling urban center located on the southwestern coast of Honshu, Japan's largest island. It was a city of cultural heritage, with ancient temples and shrines nestled among modern infrastructure. As the headquarters of the Second General Army, Hiroshima held strategic military importance, making it a key target.

On the morning of August 6, 1945, life in Hiroshima went on as usual. Residents were unaware of the impending catastrophe. At 8:15 AM, the B-29 bomber Enola Gay, piloted by Colonel Paul Tibbets, released "Little Boy," a uranium-based atomic bomb. The bomb detonated approximately 600 meters above the city, unleashing a blinding flash of light followed by an immense explosion.

The immediate impact was catastrophic. Buildings within a two-kilometer radius were obliterated, and a firestorm engulfed the city. Tens of thousands of people were killed instantly, vaporised by the intense heat or crushed by collapsing structures. Those who survived the initial blast suffered severe burns and radiation sickness. The once-thriving city was reduced to rubble, and a thick, black cloud of smoke and dust hung ominously over the ruins.

Nagasaki Before the Bomb

Nagasaki, located on the island of Kyushu, was known for its picturesque harbor and rich history of international trade. The city had a unique cultural identity, with a significant Christian community and landmarks like the Urakami Cathedral. It was also a crucial industrial center, home to the Mitsubishi shipyards and other key factories.

The original target for the second atomic bomb was Kokura. However, on August 9, 1945, the B-29 bomber Bockscar, piloted by Major Charles W. Sweeney, found Kokura obscured by clouds. After three unsuccessful bombing runs, the plane diverted to its secondary target: Nagasaki.

At 11:02 AM, "Fat Man," a plutonium-based bomb, was dropped over Nagasaki. The bomb exploded over the Urakami Valley, where many of the city's industrial facilities were located. The hilly terrain of Nagasaki somewhat contained the blast, limiting the radius of complete destruction compared to Hiroshima. Nonetheless, the devastation was immense. Approximately 40,000 people were killed instantly, with many more succumbing to injuries and radiation sickness in the following weeks.

The Immediate Aftermath in Hiroshima

The aftermath of the Hiroshima bombing was a scene of unimaginable horror. Survivors, known as hibakusha, wandered through the smouldering ruins, searching for loved ones and seeking help. The city's infrastructure was annihilated, making rescue efforts incredibly difficult. Hospitals were destroyed, and medical supplies were scarce. Those who survived the initial blast faced a dire struggle for survival in the days and weeks that followed.

As fires raged through the city, emergency responders and surviving citizens worked tirelessly to rescue the wounded. The intense heat and radiation caused severe burns, and many victims succumbed to their injuries. The water sources in Hiroshima were contaminated, leading to further suffering and deaths from dehydration and radiation poisoning. Makeshift shelters and medical stations were overwhelmed with the injured, and the sheer scale of the disaster left many without any form of aid.

The Immediate Aftermath in Nagasaki

In Nagasaki, the aftermath of the bombing was similarly devastating. The city's hilly terrain created pockets of destruction interspersed with areas that were relatively untouched. This resulted in a somewhat uneven distribution of casualties and damage. However, the destruction in the Urakami Valley was total. The bombing also severely affected the Christian community, as the Urakami Cathedral, one of the largest Christian churches in Asia, was located near the hypocenter of the blast and was completely destroyed.

Rescue efforts in Nagasaki were complicated by the geography and the extent of the devastation. Survivors faced the same dire conditions as those in Hiroshima, with severe burns, radiation sickness, and a lack of medical supplies. The psychological trauma was immense, as the survivors grappled with the loss of their homes, families, and friends. The city, like Hiroshima, was left in ruins, with a death toll that would continue to rise in the ensuing months.

Global Repercussions

The bombings of Hiroshima and Nagasaki had profound global repercussions. The sheer scale of destruction and the new, terrifying power of atomic weapons shocked the world. On August 15, 1945, just days after the bombing of Nagasaki, Japan announced its surrender, bringing World War II to an end. The bombings were a decisive factor in Japan's decision to surrender, as the leadership recognized the futility of continuing the war in the face of such overwhelming destructive power.

The use of atomic bombs also marked the beginning of the nuclear age. The bombings demonstrated the devastating potential of nuclear weapons and set the stage for the Cold War. The United States and the Soviet Union entered into an arms race, each seeking to develop more powerful and numerous nuclear arsenals. The fear of nuclear annihilation became a defining feature of international relations for the next several decades.

Rebuilding Hiroshima

The process of rebuilding Hiroshima began almost immediately, despite the immense challenges. The city was declared a City of Peace by the Japanese government, and efforts were made to reconstruct it not just physically, but also symbolically. The Hiroshima Peace Memorial, also known as the Atomic Bomb Dome, was preserved as a stark reminder of the devastation and a symbol of hope for a future without nuclear weapons.

International aid and support played a crucial role in Hiroshima's recovery. Various countries, organizations, and individuals contributed to the rebuilding efforts. Schools, hospitals, and homes were gradually reconstructed, and new infrastructure was developed. The city became a center for peace education, hosting numerous conferences and events aimed at promoting nuclear disarmament and global peace.

Every year, on August 6, Hiroshima holds a memorial ceremony to honour the victims and promote the message of peace and nuclear disarmament. The ceremony includes a moment of silence at 8:15 AM, the exact time the bomb was dropped, and the release of doves to symbolize peace.

Rebuilding Nagasaki

Nagasaki faced similar challenges in the aftermath of the bombing. The city's unique cultural heritage and international connections played a crucial role in its recovery. The Nagasaki Peace Park and the Atomic Bomb Museum were established to commemorate the victims and educate future generations about the horrors of nuclear war. The annual memorial ceremony on August 9 serves as a poignant reminder of the city's tragic past and its commitment to peace.

Rebuilding Nagasaki was a complex process. The city's hilly terrain and scattered destruction required careful planning and coordination. International aid, particularly from Christian organizations, provided vital support. The reconstruction efforts focused on restoring the city's industrial capabilities while also preserving its cultural and historical sites.

Nagasaki's Christian community, which had suffered greatly in the bombing, played a significant role in the city's recovery. The Urakami Cathedral, destroyed in the blast, was rebuilt as a symbol of resilience and hope. The survivors, or hibakusha, became powerful advocates for peace, sharing their stories and promoting nuclear disarmament.

The Legacy of the Bombings

The bombings of Hiroshima and Nagasaki left an indelible mark on the world. For the survivors, the physical and psychological scars remained a constant reminder of the horrors they endured. Many hibakusha faced discrimination and stigma, both within Japan and abroad, due to misunderstandings about radiation sickness and its effects.

The experiences of Hiroshima and Nagasaki also galvanized the global peace movement. The hibakusha became powerful advocates for nuclear disarmament, sharing their stories to raise awareness about the catastrophic consequences of nuclear warfare. Their efforts contributed to international treaties

The Science Behind the Bomb: A Journey from Theory to Devastation

The Dawn of Nuclear Physics

At the turn of the 20th century, the scientific community was on the brink of a revolution. Pioneering research into the nature of the atom was beginning to reveal secrets that would fundamentally change our understanding of the universe. Physicists like Ernest Rutherford and Niels Bohr laid the groundwork for modern atomic theory, unlocking the potential within the smallest units of matter.

It was in 1938, in a laboratory in Berlin, that the journey toward the atomic bomb truly began. German physicists Otto Hahn and Fritz Strassmann conducted an experiment that led to the discovery of nuclear fission—the process by which a heavy nucleus splits into two lighter nuclei, releasing a tremendous amount of energy. This discovery was explained by Lise Meitner and Otto Frisch, who fled Nazi Germany and communicated their findings to the broader scientific community.

Understanding Nuclear Fission

Nuclear fission occurs when the nucleus of an atom, such as uranium-235 or plutonium-239, absorbs a neutron. This absorption destabilizes the nucleus, causing it to split into two smaller nuclei, along with a few free neutrons and a large amount of energy. The released neutrons can then induce fission in other nearby nuclei, creating a chain reaction.

The energy released in nuclear fission is due to the conversion of mass into energy, as described by Albert Einstein's famous equation, $E=mc^2$. This equation implies that a small amount of mass can be converted into a large amount of energy. The potential for this energy to be harnessed in a weapon was immediately recognized by scientists around the world.

The Einstein-Szilard Letter

In the summer of 1939, physicists Leo Szilard and Eugene Wigner, both of whom had fled Europe, approached Albert Einstein with a pressing concern. They feared that Nazi Germany might be developing an atomic bomb. Einstein, a respected and influential figure, agreed to sign a letter addressed to President Franklin D. Roosevelt. This letter, delivered in October 1939, warned of the potential for a new type of bomb and urged the United States to begin its own research into nuclear fission.

President Roosevelt was initially cautious but soon established the Advisory Committee on Uranium, marking the beginning of the U.S. atomic bomb project. This project would eventually evolve into the Manhattan Project, a massive and secretive effort to develop an atomic weapon.

The Birth of the Manhattan Project

By late 1941, the United States had entered World War II, and the urgency of developing an atomic bomb intensified. The Manhattan Project, named after the Manhattan Engineer District of the U.S. Army Corps of Engineers, was established to coordinate the efforts. General Leslie Groves was appointed as the military director, and physicist J. Robert Oppenheimer was chosen to lead the scientific research.

The Manhattan Project brought together some of the greatest scientific minds of the time, including Enrico Fermi, Richard Feynman, and Niels Bohr. The project's primary research and design facility was established at Los Alamos, New Mexico, where scientists worked tirelessly to unlock the secrets of the atom and construct a functional bomb.

The Quest for Critical Mass

One of the critical challenges faced by the scientists at Los Alamos was achieving a self-sustaining chain reaction. For a nuclear explosion to occur, a certain amount of fissile material, known as the critical mass, is needed to maintain the chain reaction. If the mass of the fissile material is below this threshold, the reaction will fizzle out without releasing significant energy.

Two types of bombs were developed: a uranium-based bomb and a plutonium-based bomb. The uranium bomb, codenamed "Little Boy," used uranium-235, while the plutonium bomb, codenamed "Fat Man," used plutonium-239. The uranium-235 bomb design was relatively straightforward, involving a gun-type mechanism where two sub-critical masses of uranium were brought together to achieve critical mass.

The plutonium-239 bomb, however, required a more complex implosion mechanism. Plutonium-239 has a higher rate of spontaneous fission than uranium-235, making the gun-type design unsuitable. Instead, scientists developed an implosion design, where conventional explosives were used to compress a sub-critical sphere of plutonium into a supercritical state, triggering the chain reaction.

The Trinity Test

After years of intense research and development, the Manhattan Project reached a critical point. The first test of an atomic bomb, codenamed "Trinity," was scheduled for July 16, 1945, in the New Mexico desert. The bomb used for this test was a plutonium-239 implosion device, similar to the one later dropped on Nagasaki.

On the morning of the test, the scientists and military personnel gathered at a safe distance to witness the explosion. At precisely 5:29 AM, the bomb detonated. The explosion was more powerful than anyone had anticipated, lighting up the sky with a blinding flash and generating a mushroom cloud that rose miles into the air. The successful test confirmed that the United States now possessed a weapon of unimaginable destructive power.

Dropping the Bombs on Hiroshima and Nagasaki

With the success of the Trinity test, the stage was set for the deployment of atomic bombs in combat. The first target was Hiroshima. On August 6, 1945, the B-29 bomber Enola Gay, piloted by Colonel Paul Tibbets, dropped "Little Boy" on Hiroshima. The bomb detonated with an estimated yield of 15 kilotons of TNT, releasing a massive amount of energy in the form of heat, blast, and radiation.

The explosion caused immediate and catastrophic destruction. Buildings were vaporised, and tens of thousands of people were killed instantly. Fires spread rapidly through the city, and those who survived the initial blast faced severe burns and radiation sickness.

Three days later, on August 9, 1945, the B-29 bomber Bockscar, piloted by Major Charles W. Sweeney, dropped "Fat Man" on Nagasaki. The bomb, which had an estimated yield of 21 kilotons of TNT, detonated over the industrial district of the city. While the hilly terrain of Nagasaki somewhat contained the blast, the destruction was still immense. Approximately 40,000 people were killed instantly, with many more dying from injuries and radiation exposure in the following weeks.

The Physics Behind the Bomb

The science behind the atomic bomb is rooted in the principles of nuclear physics. At the heart of the bomb is the process of nuclear fission, where a heavy nucleus splits into two smaller nuclei, releasing energy and free neutrons. This process is initiated by bombarding the fissile material, such as uranium-235 or plutonium-239, with neutrons.

When a neutron collides with a nucleus of uranium-235 or plutonium-239, it can be absorbed, making the nucleus unstable. This instability causes the nucleus to split, forming two lighter nuclei and releasing a large amount of energy. The energy comes from the conversion of mass into energy, as described by Einstein's equation, $E=mc^2$.

The free neutrons released in the fission process can then collide with other nuclei, causing further fission events. This creates a chain reaction, which, if uncontrolled, results in an explosive release of energy. Achieving and maintaining this chain reaction requires careful engineering to ensure that enough fissile material is present and that the neutrons are properly moderated and reflected to sustain the reaction.

The Plutonium Bomb: Challenges and Innovations

The development of the plutonium bomb presented unique challenges. Plutonium-239, unlike uranium-235, has a higher rate of spontaneous fission, making it unsuitable for a gun-type design. Instead, scientists at Los Alamos devised an implosion mechanism to achieve the necessary supercritical mass.

The implosion design involved surrounding a sub-critical sphere of plutonium with conventional explosives. When detonated, these explosives created a shock wave that compressed the plutonium core, increasing its density and bringing the atoms closer together. This compression caused the plutonium to reach a supercritical state, initiating the chain reaction.

The implosion mechanism required precise engineering and synchronization of the explosive lenses to ensure uniform compression of the plutonium core. This design was successfully tested during the Trinity test, proving its viability and leading to the deployment of "Fat Man" on Nagasaki.

The Role of Uranium-235

The uranium-235 bomb, "Little Boy," used a simpler gun-type design. In this bomb, two sub-critical masses of uranium-235 were kept apart within the bomb. When detonated, a conventional explosive charge propelled one piece of uranium into the other, forming a supercritical mass and initiating the chain reaction.

The choice of uranium-235 for the first bomb was due to its availability and the relatively straightforward engineering required for the gun-type design. However, enriching uranium-235 from natural uranium, which contains mostly uranium-238, was a significant challenge. Various methods, including gaseous diffusion and electromagnetic separation, were employed to produce sufficient quantities of highly enriched uranium for the bomb.

The Aftermath and the Nuclear Age

The bombings of Hiroshima and Nagasaki marked the beginning of the nuclear age. The sheer destructive power of the atomic bombs demonstrated the potential for nuclear weapons to alter the course of history. The immediate aftermath of the bombings saw Japan's surrender, bringing an end to World War II. However, the long-term consequences of the bombings were profound and far-reaching.

The use of atomic bombs introduced a new era of military strategy and international relations. The Cold War, characterized by the nuclear arms race between the United States and the Soviet Union, dominated global politics for decades. The concept of Mutually Assured Destruction (MAD) emerged, wherein both superpowers possessed enough nuclear weapons to destroy each other many times over, creating a precarious balance of power that deterred direct conflict.

The bombings also sparked ethical debates and reflections on the use of nuclear weapons. Scientists who had worked on the Manhattan Project, such as J. Robert Oppenheimer, expressed deep moral concerns about the implications of their work. Oppenheimer famously quoted the Bhagavad Gita, saying, "Now I am become Death, the destroyer of worlds," encapsulating his inner turmoil over the weapon he helped create.

The Spread of Nuclear Technology

The success of the Manhattan Project and the subsequent use of atomic bombs led to the spread of nuclear technology. Other nations, recognizing the strategic importance of nuclear weapons, began their own research and development programs. The Soviet Union, using intelligence gathered by spies and their scientific expertise, tested their first atomic bomb in 1949, marking the start of the nuclear arms race.

The United Kingdom, France, and China also developed nuclear capabilities, joining the ranks of nuclear-armed states. The proliferation of nuclear weapons raised global concerns about the potential for catastrophic conflicts and the need for international controls to prevent the spread of nuclear technology.

Efforts Toward Disarmament and Non-Proliferation

The devastating potential of nuclear weapons prompted efforts toward disarmament and non-proliferation. In 1968, the Nuclear Non-Proliferation Treaty (NPT) was signed, aiming to prevent the spread of nuclear weapons, promote disarmament, and facilitate the peaceful use of nuclear energy. The treaty established a framework for international cooperation and verification to ensure compliance.

Despite these efforts, the challenges of nuclear proliferation persist. Nations such as India, Pakistan, and North Korea have developed nuclear weapons outside the framework of the NPT, raising regional and global security concerns. The threat of nuclear terrorism also looms, as non-state actors seek to acquire nuclear materials for malicious purposes.

The Legacy of the Manhattan Project

The Manhattan Project, one of the most ambitious scientific endeavours in history, left a complex legacy. On one hand, it demonstrated the incredible potential of scientific collaboration and innovation. The project brought together brilliant minds from diverse backgrounds to solve unprecedented technical challenges, leading to significant advancements in physics, engineering, and technology.

On the other hand, the Manhattan Project also highlighted the ethical dilemmas and moral responsibilities associated with scientific research. The development and use of atomic bombs resulted in immense human suffering and environmental devastation. The legacy of the Manhattan Project serves as a reminder of the need to carefully consider the implications of scientific discoveries and their potential impact on humanity.

Reflections on the Atomic Age

The science behind the atomic bomb, from the discovery of nuclear fission to the deployment of the bombs on Hiroshima and Nagasaki, is a story of both triumph and tragedy. It showcases the power of human ingenuity and the relentless pursuit of knowledge, but also the destructive potential that comes with such advancements.

As we continue to navigate the challenges of the nuclear age, the lessons of the past remain critically important. The horrors of Hiroshima and Nagasaki, the ethical debates among scientists, and the ongoing efforts toward disarmament and non-proliferation all underscore the need for responsible stewardship of nuclear technology.

The story of the atomic bomb is a powerful testament to the dual-edged nature of scientific progress. It reminds us that with great power comes great responsibility, and that the pursuit of knowledge must always be tempered by a commitment to ethical principles and the well-being of humanity

# CHAPTER FIFTEEN

# Criteria for Choosing Targets for the Atomic Bombs

The selection of targets for the atomic bombs during World War II was a meticulous and strategic process involving various military and political considerations. The goal was to force Japan's surrender by demonstrating overwhelming destructive power while also maximizing military impact. Here are the primary criteria used in selecting the targets:

1. Military Significance

Industrial and Military Facilities: Targets needed to have significant military value, such as being centers of war production or having major military installations. The aim was to cripple Japan's war-making capacity by destroying critical infrastructure.

Troop Concentrations: Areas with significant military personnel or logistical hubs were preferred to disrupt Japan's ability to defend itself or continue the war effort.

2. Psychological Impact

High Population Density: Cities with large populations were considered because the destruction of a populous area would have a greater psychological impact on both the Japanese leadership and the civilian population.

Demonstration of Power: The targets needed to be chosen to effectively demonstrate the bomb's unprecedented destructive power, which would hopefully compel Japan to surrender.

3. Urban Environment

Intact Urban Areas: Cities that had been relatively untouched by conventional bombing were preferred. This allowed for a clearer assessment of the atomic bomb's impact and ensured that the bombing would be a dramatic demonstration of power.

Urban Density: Dense urban environments would maximize the bomb's destructive potential, causing widespread devastation and thereby enhancing the psychological impact.

4. Weather Conditions

Clear Weather: Favourable weather conditions were crucial. Clear skies ensured the bomb could be accurately dropped, maximizing its effectiveness. On the day of the mission, target selection could be influenced by real-time weather observations.

Visual Bombing: The bomb needed to be dropped visually, which meant clear visibility was essential. This was to ensure the bomb detonated at the planned altitude and location for maximum effect.

5. Strategic and Tactical Considerations

Multiple Targets: Having multiple potential targets ensured that if conditions were not favourable for one city, another could be bombed instead. This flexibility was crucial for the success of the mission.

Avoiding Duplication of Effect: The targets were chosen to ensure a broad demonstration of the bomb's capabilities across different environments and to avoid unnecessary duplication of damage to similar types of targets.

6. Political Considerations

Minimizing Long-term Hostility: There were concerns about the long-term consequences of targeting certain cities. For instance, Kyoto was removed from the list due to its cultural and historical significance, and the potential backlash such a strike could engender post-war.

International Perception: The choice of targets also considered how the bombings would be viewed internationally, especially by allies and neutral countries. There was a desire to maintain moral high ground and justify the use of such a devastating weapon.

The Process of Target Selection

The process of selecting targets for the atomic bombs involved several key figures and groups, including military planners, scientists from the Manhattan Project, and senior political leaders.

Target Committee Meetings: The Target Committee, led by Major General Leslie Groves and including scientists like J. Robert Oppenheimer, held meetings to discuss potential targets. They considered factors such as military value, potential for destruction, and psychological impact.

Initial List of Targets: The initial list of potential targets included Hiroshima, Kokura, Nagasaki, and Kyoto. These cities were chosen based on the criteria outlined above, with considerations for their military significance, urban density, and psychological impact.

Removal of Kyoto: Secretary of War Henry Stimson played a pivotal role in the removal of Kyoto from the target list. Stimson appreciated Kyoto's cultural and historical importance and argued that its destruction would not only obliterate a significant part of Japanese heritage but also hinder post-war reconciliation efforts. His insistence led to the substitution of Nagasaki as a target.

Final Decision: The final decision on the targets was made with input from both military and political leaders, including President Harry S. Truman. Hiroshima was chosen as the first target due to its military importance and relatively untouched state, which would allow for a clear demonstration of the bomb's power. Nagasaki, initially a secondary target, was selected due to its industrial significance and the unfavourable conditions over Kokura on the day of the bombing.

The selection of targets for the atomic bombs was a complex process influenced by a range of military, psychological, and political factors. The ultimate goal was to force Japan's surrender and end World War II swiftly while demonstrating the overwhelming power of the new weapon. The careful consideration of these criteria reflects the gravity of the decision and the profound impact it had on the course of history.

# CHAPTER SIXTEEN

# The Decision to Bomb Nagasaki: A Story of Strategy and Survival

The Decision to Bomb Nagasaki: A Story of Strategy and Survival

The Shadow of War

In the summer of 1945, the world was embroiled in the final throes of World War II. The European theater had concluded with the unconditional surrender of Nazi Germany in May, but the war in the Pacific continued to rage. Japan, though battered and nearly defeated, showed no signs of surrender. The United States faced a formidable challenge: how to bring the war to a swift and decisive end without the need for a costly and bloody invasion of the Japanese mainland.

The United States had developed a powerful new weapon, the atomic bomb, through the top-secret Manhattan Project. The bomb's potential to end the war quickly and decisively was clear, but the decision to use it was fraught with moral, strategic, and political complexities.

The Birth of the Manhattan Project

The Manhattan Project had its roots in the early days of World War II. In 1939, scientists Albert Einstein and Leo Szilard wrote a letter to President Franklin D. Roosevelt, warning that Nazi Germany was researching nuclear weapons. This letter spurred the

U.S. government to initiate its own atomic research program. Over the next few years, under the direction of General Leslie Groves and physicist J. Robert Oppenheimer, the project grew into a massive undertaking involving thousands of scientists, engineers, and workers.

By 1945, the project had reached its culmination. On July 16, 1945, the first atomic bomb was successfully tested in the New Mexico desert. The test, codenamed "Trinity," produced a blinding flash and a mushroom cloud that rose 40,000 feet into the sky. The bomb had demonstrated its devastating power, and now the decision on how to use it rested with the highest levels of the U.S. government.

The Target Committee Meetings

The process of selecting targets for the atomic bombs began with the establishment of the Target Committee. This group, chaired by General Groves, included top scientists like Oppenheimer, military strategists, and political advisors. Their task was to identify potential targets that would maximize the bomb's impact and compel Japan to surrender.

Meeting in Washington, D.C.

In the spring of 1945, the Target Committee convened in Washington, D.C. The atmosphere was tense, as the weight of their decisions was palpable. General Groves opened the meeting by outlining the criteria for target selection: military significance, potential for destruction, and psychological impact.

"We need to choose targets that will not only cripple Japan's war-making capacity but also shock them into surrendering," Groves said, his voice firm and resolute.

Oppenheimer, the scientific mind behind the bomb, added, "The cities we select should be relatively untouched by previous bombings. This will allow us to assess the full impact of the atomic bomb."

The committee members nodded in agreement. They began by listing several cities that met these criteria: Hiroshima, Kokura, Nagasaki, and Kyoto.

The Case for Hiroshima

Hiroshima quickly emerged as a top contender. It was a major industrial city with significant military installations. Its dense population would ensure that the bomb's impact would be devastating, both materially and psychologically.

"Destroying Hiroshima would send a clear message," Groves asserted. "It's a city that symbolizes Japan's war effort."

The committee agreed, and Hiroshima was placed at the top of the list.

Kyoto: A Cultural Treasure

Kyoto was another city under consideration. It was an important industrial center and had a large population. However, it was also Japan's cultural and historical heart, home to thousands of temples, shrines, and historical buildings.

As the committee discussed Kyoto, Henry Stimson, the Secretary of War, intervened. Stimson had visited Kyoto before the war and was deeply moved by its beauty and cultural significance.

"Kyoto is not just another city," Stimson argued passionately. "It's the cultural soul of Japan. Destroying it would not only obliterate a significant part of Japanese heritage but also make post-war reconciliation nearly impossible."

Groves and other committee members listened intently. Stimson's argument was compelling, and the thought of destroying such a cultural treasure weighed heavily on their minds.

Further Discussions and Revisions

Over the next few meetings, the committee continued to deliberate. Groves, despite his initial inclination, began to see the merit in Stimson's argument. The decision to remove Kyoto from the target list was not taken lightly, but ultimately, it was agreed upon. The cultural and political ramifications of bombing Kyoto were deemed too great.

With Kyoto off the list, the focus shifted to the remaining cities: Hiroshima, Kokura, and Nagasaki. Each city had its own strategic importance, and the committee refined their plans based on further military and meteorological assessments.

The Final Decision

The final decision on the targets involved not just the Target Committee but also the highest echelons of the U.S. government. President Harry S. Truman, who had assumed office after Roosevelt's death in April 1945, was deeply involved in the discussions. Truman was aware of the immense power of the atomic bomb and the moral implications of using it.

In a series of meetings with his advisors, Truman weighed the options. He listened to General Groves, Stimson, Oppenheimer, and others as they presented their recommendations. The consensus was clear: the atomic bomb could force Japan to surrender and save countless lives that would otherwise be lost in a prolonged war.

On July 25, 1945, Truman gave the final authorization to use the bomb. Hiroshima was to be the first target, with Kokura and Nagasaki as subsequent targets. The decision was made with a heavy heart but with the belief that it would bring about the end of the war.

The Bombing of Hiroshima

On August 6, 1945, the B-29 bomber Enola Gay, piloted by Colonel Paul Tibbets, took off from Tinian Island in the Pacific. Its mission was to drop the atomic bomb, codenamed "Little Boy," on Hiroshima. The bomb detonated at 8:15 AM, unleashing a blast equivalent to 15,000 tons of TNT. The explosion obliterated much of the city, killing tens of thousands instantly and causing immense destruction.

The impact of the bombing was beyond comprehension. Survivors described scenes of unimaginable horror: bodies charred beyond recognition, buildings reduced to rubble, and a city engulfed in flames. The psychological shockwaves were felt across Japan, but the government did not immediately surrender.

The Second Bombing: Nagasaki

Three days later, on August 9, 1945, a second atomic bomb was ready. This time, the B-29 bomber Bockscar, piloted by Major Charles W. Sweeney, was tasked with delivering the bomb, codenamed "Fat Man," to Kokura. However, when Bockscar approached Kokura, the city was shrouded in clouds and smoke from previous bombings, making visual targeting impossible.

With fuel running low, Sweeney made the decision to divert to the secondary target: Nagasaki. At 11:02 AM, the bomb was dropped over the city. The explosion was even more powerful than the first, equivalent to 21,000 tons of TNT. The hilly terrain of Nagasaki somewhat contained the blast, but the destruction was still catastrophic. An estimated 70,000 people were killed by the end of 1945, with many more suffering from injuries and radiation sickness.

The Aftermath and Surrender

The twin bombings of Hiroshima and Nagasaki had a profound psychological impact on Japan's leadership. Coupled with the Soviet Union's declaration of war against Japan on August 8, and their subsequent invasion of Japanese-held territories in Manchuria, the situation became untenable for Japan.

Emperor Hirohito, who had been largely a figurehead during the war, took the unprecedented step of intervening directly. Recognizing the futility of continued resistance and the devastating consequences of further atomic bombings, he urged the Japanese government to accept the terms of the Potsdam Declaration.

On August 15, 1945, Hirohito announced Japan's surrender in a radio broadcast. His voice, calm yet somber, reached the ears of millions of Japanese citizens who had never heard their Emperor speak before. The war was over, but the scars left by the atomic bombings would endure for generations.

Reflections and Legacy

The decision to use the atomic bombs on Hiroshima and Nagasaki remains one of the most controversial and debated actions in military history. While it achieved its immediate objective of ending World War II, it also unleashed unprecedented destruction and suffering. The bombings left deep scars on the cities and their inhabitants, and the ethical implications of using such a weapon continue to provoke intense debate.

The sparing of Kyoto, however, stands as a testament to the consideration of cultural and historical values even in the midst of war. The city's survival allowed it to continue its role as a custodian of Japanese tradition and a source of national pride. It also facilitated post-war reconciliation, helping to rebuild trust between Japan and the United States.

The story of why Nagasaki was chosen over Kyoto, Kokura, and other cities is a complex narrative of military strategy, political deliberation, and ethical considerations. The decisions made in those crucial months of 1945 were guided by the goal of ending the war swiftly while also weighing the long-term consequences.

The legacy of these decisions is profound. Hiroshima and Nagasaki bear the memories of destruction and resilience, while Kyoto stands as a symbol of cultural preservation. The choices made by leaders like Henry Stimson, General Leslie Groves, and President Harry S. Truman continue to resonate, reminding us of the delicate balance between military necessity and humanitarian values .

# Thank God Kyoto Survived: The Unchosen Target

The Historical and Cultural Jewel

Nestled in a valley surrounded by mountains, Kyoto was once the heart of Japan. As the imperial capital for over a thousand years, from 794 to 1868, it had witnessed the rise and fall of empires, the blooming of arts, and the shaping of Japan's spiritual and cultural identity. Its streets were adorned with thousands of temples and shrines, ancient wooden houses, and serene gardens that whispered stories of a glorious past.

Kyoto was a living museum, a repository of Japan's most treasured artefacts and traditions. The Kinkaku-ji, or Golden Pavilion, shimmered in the sunlight beside its reflecting pond, while the Kiyomizu-dera temple, perched on a hillside, offered breathtaking views of cherry blossoms in spring and crimson leaves in autumn. The city's historical significance was unparalleled, making it a symbol of Japan's rich heritage.

The Looming Threat of Destruction

As World War II raged on, the United States sought a way to bring the conflict in the Pacific to a swift and decisive end. The development of the atomic bomb under the Manhattan Project provided a new, fearsome weapon that could potentially force

Japan's surrender without a costly invasion. Military strategists began to identify potential targets for the bomb, focusing on cities that held strategic, industrial, and psychological significance.

Among the initial targets considered for the atomic bombings were Hiroshima, Nagasaki, Kokura, and Kyoto. Despite its cultural and historical significance, Kyoto was listed as a potential target due to its population size and its industrial contributions to the war effort. The thought of Kyoto's ancient temples and cultural treasures reduced to ashes was a grim prospect.

The Intervention of Henry Stimson

Henry Stimson, the U.S. Secretary of War, played a crucial role in the decision-making process regarding the atomic bomb targets. Stimson had a deep appreciation for history and culture, and he had visited Kyoto years earlier, experiencing firsthand the city's profound beauty and historical importance. He understood that Kyoto was not just another city; it was the cultural soul of Japan.

Stimson believed that the destruction of Kyoto would not only obliterate a priceless heritage but also have long-term negative consequences for post-war relations between the United States and Japan. He argued vehemently against targeting Kyoto, emphasizing that its cultural significance far outweighed any military advantages that might be gained from its destruction.

The Decision-Making Process

In the war rooms where military and political leaders debated the targets for the atomic bombs, Stimson's voice was persistent and persuasive. He appealed to President Harry S. Truman and other key figures, highlighting Kyoto's historical and cultural value. Stimson's respect for Kyoto's legacy and his foresight about the post-war implications were critical in shaping the final decision.

General Leslie Groves, the military director of the Manhattan Project, had initially supported the inclusion of Kyoto on the target list due to its population and industrial facilities. However, after several discussions and Stimson's unwavering stance, Groves and others began to reconsider. The argument that the destruction of Kyoto would severely damage Japan's cultural fabric and make post-war reconciliation more difficult ultimately swayed the decision-makers.

In the end, President Truman and his advisors decided to remove Kyoto from the list of potential targets. Hiroshima, Nagasaki, and Kokura remained, but Kyoto was spared. The decision was not just a military one; it was a recognition of the profound human and cultural loss that would have accompanied the city's destruction.

The Aftermath and Reflections

On August 6, 1945, the atomic bomb was dropped on Hiroshima, followed by the bombing of Nagasaki on August 9. The devastation was immense, and Japan surrendered shortly thereafter, bringing an end to World War II. While the war's conclusion was a relief, the horror of the atomic bombings left a deep scar on the global conscience.

In the years that followed, as Japan rebuilt and the world reflected on the war's devastation, the survival of Kyoto became a symbol of hope and resilience. The city continued to be a beacon of Japan's cultural and historical heritage, its temples and gardens offering solace and inspiration.

Kyoto's survival allowed it to remain a center for cultural preservation and education. Scholars and tourists from around the world visited the city to experience its unique blend of history, art, and spirituality. The decision to spare Kyoto became a poignant reminder of the importance of protecting cultural treasures even amidst the horrors of war.

The Legacy of the Decision

The sparing of Kyoto had significant implications for post-war relations between the United States and Japan. It demonstrated a respect for Japanese culture and history, which helped to facilitate reconciliation and the rebuilding of trust between the two nations. The preservation of Kyoto allowed it to continue its role as a custodian of Japanese tradition and a source of national pride.

In the broader context, the decision highlighted the importance of considering cultural heritage in military strategy. The destruction of cultural sites during war is a loss not only for the affected country but for humanity as a whole. Kyoto's survival serves as a testament to the value of cultural preservation and the importance of making ethical decisions even in the midst of conflict.

Today, Kyoto stands as a living testament to Japan's rich history and cultural legacy. Its ancient temples, serene gardens, and traditional festivals continue to draw visitors from around the world. The city's survival is celebrated as a triumph of cultural preservation and a reminder of the power of compassion and foresight in decision-making.

The story of Kyoto's survival is a remarkable tale of how the appreciation of culture and history can influence critical decisions in times of war. Thanks to the efforts of individuals like Henry Stimson, the world retains a priceless cultural treasure that continues to inspire and educate generations. Kyoto's spared existence underscores the profound impact that such decisions can have on shaping the cultural and historical legacy of nations. The phrase "Thank God Kyoto Survived" resonates deeply, reminding us of the enduring importance of safeguarding our shared human heritage.

# CHAPTER EIGHTEEN

# Global Reactions and Implications: The Aftermath of Nagasaki

The morning of August 9, 1945, when Nagasaki was decimated by the second atomic bomb, the world witnessed an unprecedented level of destruction and the dawn of a new era in warfare. As the news spread, the global reaction was swift and multifaceted, encompassing shock, horror, political calculations, and ethical debates. The bombings of Hiroshima and Nagasaki did not just end World War II; they also sparked a profound shift in international relations, military strategy, and public consciousness.

The immediate reports from Nagasaki were harrowing. Journalists who arrived at the scene described a city annihilated, with survivors wandering through the ruins, suffering from burns and radiation sickness. John Hersey's vivid accounts in The New Yorker provided a human face to the abstract horror, detailing the experiences of hibakusha and capturing the global audience's imagination. His portrayal of the suffering and resilience of the survivors elicited a wave of empathy and moral outrage worldwide.

As images of the devastation reached newspapers and radio broadcasts, the world began to grapple with the implications of atomic warfare. Media outlets across the globe featured stark photographs of the mushroom clouds and the flattened cities.

Headlines screamed about the new, terrifying power of nuclear weapons. The initial reaction in many Western countries, particularly the United States and the Allied nations, was a mixture of relief and triumph. The atomic bomb had succeeded in forcing Japan's surrender, potentially saving countless lives that would have been lost in a prolonged war.

President Harry S. Truman addressed the American public with a speech that underscored the necessity of using the atomic bomb to end the war swiftly. He spoke of the bomb as a powerful new weapon that could prevent future conflicts, framing it as a means of achieving lasting peace. However, even within the United States, there were voices of dissent. Scientists from the Manhattan Project, such as Leo Szilard and James Franck, had previously expressed their concerns about the ethical implications of using such a weapon on civilian populations.

In the United Kingdom, Prime Minister Winston Churchill echoed Truman's sentiments, emphasizing the bomb's role in bringing a swift conclusion to the war. Yet, the bombings also sparked a debate among British intellectuals and politicians about the future of warfare and the moral responsibilities of those who possessed nuclear capabilities. The British press was filled with both support for the decision and a growing unease about the implications of nuclear arms.

The reaction in the Soviet Union was one of mixed emotions. While publicly expressing solidarity with the Allied decision, Soviet Premier Joseph Stalin was deeply concerned about the strategic balance of power. The successful use of the atomic bomb by the United States highlighted a significant technological gap that the Soviets were eager to close. This realization accelerated the Soviet Union's own nuclear program, marking the beginning of the Cold War arms race.

In Japan, the bombings of Hiroshima and Nagasaki led to profound national trauma and introspection. Emperor Hirohito's unprecedented radio address announcing Japan's surrender acknowledged the "new and most cruel bomb" as a decisive factor.

The Japanese people, already weary from years of war and hardship, were plunged into a period of mourning and reflection. The devastation wrought by the bombs, combined with the subsequent American occupation, fundamentally reshaped Japanese society and politics.

Reactions from other parts of the world varied. In Europe, nations recovering from the devastation of the war were both horrified and fascinated by the destructive power of the atomic bomb. Countries like France and Germany, while focusing on their own reconstruction, began to consider the implications of nuclear technology for future conflicts. In Asia, countries under Japanese occupation or influence saw the bombings as a dramatic end to imperial aggression, yet were also wary of the new era of American dominance.

Global religious leaders also weighed in. Pope Pius XII condemned the use of atomic bombs, calling for a return to Christian values and the pursuit of peace through non-violent means. Religious leaders across different faiths echoed similar sentiments, emphasizing the moral and ethical considerations that should guide the use of such powerful weapons.

The ethical and moral debates that emerged from the bombings were intense and far-reaching. Philosophers, theologians, and public intellectuals engaged in vigorous discussions about the justification and consequences of using atomic bombs. The concept of just war theory was scrutinized in light of the unprecedented civilian casualties and long-term suffering caused by radiation.

The bombings of Hiroshima and Nagasaki also galvanized the global peace movement. Anti-nuclear activists, many inspired by the hibakusha's testimonies, campaigned tirelessly for nuclear disarmament. Figures like Albert Einstein and Bertrand Russell became vocal advocates for the abolition of nuclear weapons. The Russell-Einstein Manifesto of 1955 called for an end to nuclear weapons and a focus on peaceful resolution of conflicts, influencing public opinion and policy discussions worldwide.

The establishment of the United Nations in 1945 provided a new platform for addressing global security issues. The bombings underscored the urgent need for international cooperation to prevent the proliferation of nuclear weapons. The first resolution adopted by the UN General Assembly in January 1946 called for the elimination of atomic weapons and the use of atomic energy only for peaceful purposes. This resolution laid the groundwork for future non-proliferation efforts.

The geopolitical landscape was irrevocably altered by the introduction of nuclear weapons. The United States and the Soviet Union emerged as superpowers, each possessing the capability to annihilate the other. The ensuing arms race saw both nations amassing vast arsenals of nuclear weapons, leading to a precarious balance of power known as Mutually Assured Destruction (MAD). This doctrine, while preventing direct conflict between the superpowers, created a tense global atmosphere marked by fear and suspicion.

The nuclear arms race prompted significant scientific and technological advancements. Both the United States and the Soviet Union invested heavily in research and development, leading to innovations in missile technology, electronics, and other fields. However, this rapid technological progress came with the constant threat of nuclear annihilation, profoundly affecting the collective psyche of the global population.

In the decades following the bombings, efforts toward nuclear disarmament and non-proliferation gained momentum. The Nuclear Non-Proliferation Treaty (NPT) of 1968, signed by numerous countries, aimed to prevent the spread of nuclear weapons and promote disarmament. Despite challenges and setbacks, the treaty represented a significant step toward global cooperation in addressing the threat of nuclear warfare.

The impact of the bombings on Nagasaki and Hiroshima also led to a reevaluation of the principles of international humanitarian law. The Geneva Conventions, which set the standards for the treatment of civilians and combatants during war, were revisited with a focus on the protection of civilian populations in the age of nuclear weapons. The concept of war crimes and crimes against humanity gained prominence, influencing subsequent international legal frameworks.

The legacy of Nagasaki and Hiroshima extends beyond the realm of geopolitics and international law. The bombings have deeply influenced art, literature, and culture. Writers, filmmakers, and artists have grappled with the profound implications of nuclear warfare, creating works that explore themes of destruction, survival, and the human condition. John Hersey's Hiroshima, Kenzaburo Oe's Hiroshima Notes, and films like Grave of the Fireflies and Barefoot Gen are poignant examples of how the atomic bombings have been memorialized in cultural memory.

The hibakusha's testimonies and the global peace movement have had a lasting impact on public consciousness. Educational programs and initiatives, such as the Hiroshima Peace Memorial Museum and the Nagasaki Atomic Bomb Museum, play a crucial role in teaching future generations about the horrors of nuclear war and the importance of peace. Annual memorial ceremonies in both cities serve as a reminder of the past and a call to action for a nuclear-free world.

As we reflect on the global reactions and implications of the Nagasaki bombing, it is clear that the event has shaped the course of history in profound ways. The introduction of nuclear weapons changed the dynamics of international relations, spurred efforts toward disarmament, and ignited ethical debates that continue to resonate today. The story of Nagasaki is not just a tale of destruction but also a testament to the enduring human spirit and the global commitment to peace and justice.

# Role of Nagasaki in Ending WWII

On the morning of August 9, 1945, the city of Nagasaki awoke to the familiar sounds of wartime. Air raid sirens had become a routine part of life, warning residents of the potential for bombing raids. However, this day was destined to be unlike any other. High above the city, unseen by those on the ground, the B-29 bomber Bockscar was approaching, carrying a weapon of unprecedented destructive power.

Nagasaki, a city known for its beautiful harbour and its mix of Japanese and Western influences, had become an important industrial center during the war. Its shipyards, steelworks, and armament factories were critical to Japan's war effort. Yet, for all its strategic importance, Nagasaki was not initially the primary target for the second atomic bomb. That dubious honour belonged to the city of Kokura.

As Bockscar neared Kokura, the crew found the city obscured by clouds and smoke from previous bombings. With visibility too poor for an accurate drop, the decision was made to proceed to the secondary target: Nagasaki. At 11:02 AM, the atomic bomb, codenamed "Fat Man," was released. It detonated over the Urakami Valley, a densely populated area with significant industrial facilities.

The explosion was cataclysmic. A blinding flash of light was followed by a massive blast, levelling buildings and incinerating everything within a two-mile radius. The intense heat ignited fires throughout the city, and a towering mushroom cloud rose into the sky. Approximately 40,000 people were killed instantly, and countless others suffered horrific injuries and radiation sickness.

In the immediate aftermath, the city was plunged into chaos. Survivors, many of them horribly burned and injured, wandered through the ruins in shock. Hospitals were overwhelmed, and medical supplies were woefully inadequate. The once-thriving city was reduced to a hellscape of twisted metal and ash, with the cries of the injured and dying filling the air.

But the impact of the bombing of Nagasaki extended far beyond the immediate devastation. In Tokyo, the Japanese government had been grappling with the reality of their untenable position. The destruction of Hiroshima just three days earlier had already sent shockwaves through the leadership, but there was still hesitation and debate about whether to surrender.

The bombing of Nagasaki forced a decisive shift. The Japanese military had been deeply divided on the question of surrender. Some high-ranking officers were determined to continue fighting, believing that Japan could still negotiate better terms. Others recognized the futility of further resistance in the face of such overwhelming power. The combined impact of two atomic bombs, along with the Soviet Union's declaration of war on Japan and invasion of Manchuria on August 8, created a situation that could no longer be ignored.

Emperor Hirohito, who had been largely a symbolic figurehead during the war, took an unprecedented step. On August 14, after days of intense discussion and the urging of key advisors, he made the decision to intervene directly. In a historic broadcast to the nation on August 15, Hirohito announced Japan's surrender, citing the devastating power of the atomic bombs and the need to save the Japanese people from further suffering.

The announcement marked the end of World War II, bringing a sense of relief to a world weary of conflict. However, it also marked the beginning of a long and painful period of reflection for Japan. The use of atomic bombs on Hiroshima and Nagasaki was seen by many as a necessary evil to end the war quickly and save lives that would have been lost in a protracted invasion. Yet, for the people of Nagasaki, the cost was immeasurable.

The role of Nagasaki in ending World War II is a complex and multifaceted story. The city's destruction underscored the devastating capabilities of nuclear weapons and the grim reality of modern warfare. It highlighted the desperate final days of the Japanese war effort, where the hope for a negotiated peace was eclipsed by the brutal calculus of total war.

In the years following the war, Nagasaki, like Hiroshima, became a symbol of peace and resilience. The city's journey from ruin to recovery was marked by the determination of its people to rebuild and to ensure that the horrors of nuclear war were never forgotten. The Nagasaki Peace Park and the Atomic Bomb Museum stand as testaments to this commitment, offering a place of reflection and learning for visitors from around the world.

The stories of the survivors, the hibakusha, became a vital part of this narrative. Their testimonies provided a human face to the abstract horrors of nuclear war, reminding the world of the real and lasting impact of these weapons. Their voices were instrumental in the global movement for nuclear disarmament, advocating for a world where such devastation could never happen again.

Nagasaki's role in ending World War II also influenced international relations and policy. The bombings prompted a reevaluation of military strategy and the ethics of using such powerful weapons. The fear of nuclear annihilation that followed led to the Cold War arms race, but also to efforts aimed at controlling and eventually eliminating nuclear weapons.

As the decades passed, the legacy of Nagasaki continued to shape global discourse on peace and security. The annual memorial ceremonies, held every August 9, serve as a reminder of the past and a call to action for the future. Leaders from around the world attend these ceremonies, reflecting on the lessons of history and reaffirming their commitment to peace.

In the grand tapestry of World War II, the bombing of Nagasaki was a pivotal moment. It brought the war to a close, but at an unimaginable cost. The city's destruction served as a powerful warning of the dangers of nuclear warfare and the need for vigilance and restraint in the use of such weapons.

Today, Nagasaki stands as a beacon of hope and resilience. Its rebuilt streets and thriving communities are a testament to the strength and determination of its people. The city's commitment to peace and education continues to inspire future generations, ensuring that the lessons of the past are never forgotten.

The story of Nagasaki is not just about the end of a war; it is about the enduring human spirit and the quest for a better, safer world. It is a story that reminds us of the profound impact of our actions and the importance of striving for peace, even in the face of the darkest .

# CHAPTER TWENTY

# Hibakusha Testimonies

On a warm August morning in 1945, the residents of Nagasaki went about their daily routines, unaware that their lives were about to change forever. Among them was a young girl named Keiko, who lived with her family in a modest home near the Urakami Cathedral. Keiko's father worked at the Mitsubishi shipyards, while her mother tended their small garden and cared for Keiko and her younger brother, Hiroshi.

That morning, Keiko walked to school, her thoughts filled with the upcoming end-of-term exams. She met her friends along the way, and they chatted and laughed, oblivious to the approaching catastrophe. As the clock struck 11:02 AM, the sky above Nagasaki was torn apart by a blinding flash of light, followed by a deafening explosion. The atomic bomb, codenamed "Fat Man," had detonated over the city.

Keiko was thrown to the ground by the force of the blast. She felt a searing heat and then darkness. When she regained consciousness, the world around her had transformed into a nightmarish landscape. Buildings were reduced to rubble, and the air was filled with smoke and ash. The cries of the injured and dying echoed through the streets.

Keiko stumbled through the debris, her body covered in burns, searching for her family. She found her school reduced to ruins, her friends nowhere to be seen. She continued her desperate search, eventually finding her home destroyed. Her parents and brother were among the countless victims who had perished in the blast.

Years later, Keiko would become one of the many hibakusha, or atomic bomb survivors, who would share their stories with the world. Her testimony, like those of others, was a powerful reminder of the horrors of nuclear warfare and the resilience of the human spirit.

Sumiteru Taniguchi was another survivor whose story became emblematic of the hibakusha experience. At the time of the bombing, Sumiteru was a 16-year-old boy delivering mail on his bicycle. When the bomb exploded, he was thrown to the ground, his back exposed to the intense heat and radiation. His skin was severely burned, and he lay in the rubble for hours before being rescued.

Sumiteru's injuries were so severe that he spent the next 21 months in a hospital, undergoing multiple surgeries and enduring excruciating pain. Despite his suffering, he found the strength to become an advocate for nuclear disarmament. He travelled the world, speaking at conferences and sharing his story with anyone who would listen. His testimony was a stark reminder of the human cost of nuclear weapons and a call to action for a world free from their threat.

Another poignant testimony came from a man named Shigeko Sasamori. She was a teenager at the time of the bombing, living with her family in Nagasaki. The explosion left her with severe burns and injuries. Shigeko spent years in and out of hospitals, undergoing numerous surgeries to repair the damage to her body.

Despite the physical and emotional scars, Shigeko dedicated her life to peace activism. She moved to the United States, where she continued her education and became a nurse. Shigeko joined the Hiroshima Maidens, a group of young women who had survived the bombings and travelled to the U.S. for reconstructive surgery. Together, they shared their experiences and advocated for nuclear disarmament.

One of the most haunting stories came from a man named Kiyoshi Tanimoto. A Methodist minister in Hiroshima, Tanimoto was in the city center when the bomb exploded. He survived the blast and immediately began helping others, pulling injured people from the rubble and offering comfort to the dying.

In the years that followed, Tanimoto became a prominent figure in the anti-nuclear movement. He travelled to the United States, where he met with political leaders and appeared on television to share his story. His efforts were instrumental in raising awareness about the horrors of nuclear warfare and the need for disarmament.

The hibakusha's testimonies were not only accounts of the physical and emotional devastation caused by the atomic bombings but also powerful calls for peace and reconciliation. These survivors, bearing the scars of their past, became symbols of hope and resilience. Their stories transcended borders and cultures, reminding the world of the shared humanity and the imperative to prevent such tragedies from ever occurring again.

Each testimony was unique, yet they all shared common themes of suffering, loss, and an unyielding spirit. The hibakusha spoke of the intense heat and blinding light of the explosion, the immediate chaos and destruction, and the long-term health effects of radiation exposure. They recounted their struggles to rebuild their lives amidst the ruins and their determination to ensure that future generations would not endure the same horrors.

Their voices were often filled with sorrow but also with a profound sense of purpose. The hibakusha understood that their stories were not just personal accounts but vital contributions to a global narrative about the dangers of nuclear weapons. They spoke for those who could no longer speak, honouring the memory of the countless lives lost.

Through their testimonies, the hibakusha helped to humanize the abstract concept of nuclear warfare. They provided a visceral, firsthand perspective on the consequences of these weapons, challenging policymakers and citizens alike to consider the moral and ethical implications of their use.

The legacy of the hibakusha is one of courage and compassion. Their stories have been instrumental in the global movement for nuclear disarmament, influencing treaties and agreements aimed at reducing and eventually eliminating nuclear arsenals. They have inspired countless individuals and organizations to join the fight for a world free from the threat of nuclear annihilation.

As the years pass and the number of surviving hibakusha dwindles, their testimonies remain a crucial part of our collective memory. Efforts to preserve their stories through oral histories, documentaries, and educational programs continue, ensuring that future generations understand the gravity of the atomic bombings and the importance of pursuing peace.

The hibakusha's voices remind us that the true cost of war is measured not in abstract statistics but in the lives of individuals and families. Their experiences serve as a powerful testament to the resilience of the human spirit and the enduring hope for a world where peace prevails over conflict.

# CHAPTER TWENTY-ONE

# Nagasaki Reborn: The Story of Reconstruction and Recovery

In the aftermath of the atomic bombing on August 9, 1945, Nagasaki lay in ruins. The once-vibrant city, known for its bustling ports, lush hills, and rich cultural tapestry, was reduced to rubble and ash. The devastation was total: buildings obliterated, infrastructure destroyed, and thousands of lives lost. For the survivors, the immediate future was a bleak and daunting landscape of destruction and despair. Yet, from this desolation, Nagasaki would rise again, embodying resilience, hope, and the human spirit's capacity for renewal.

The first days and weeks after the bombing were a harrowing struggle for survival. The survivors, many of them grievously injured and suffering from radiation sickness, faced a dire lack of medical supplies, food, and clean water. Makeshift shelters were set up amidst the ruins, and the few remaining hospitals were overwhelmed with the wounded. International aid was slow to arrive, and the full extent of the devastation made coordinated relief efforts incredibly challenging.

Despite these overwhelming obstacles, the people of Nagasaki began the arduous task of rebuilding their lives. The city's immediate recovery efforts were spearheaded by local authorities and community leaders who organized search and rescue missions, cleared debris, and established temporary housing for the displaced. Volunteers from neighbouring regions and other parts of Japan arrived to assist in these efforts, bringing much-needed supplies and support.

The Japanese government, recognizing the symbolic importance of Nagasaki and Hiroshima, committed to reconstructing the cities not only as physical spaces but also as symbols of peace and resilience. Reconstruction efforts were planned meticulously, with a focus on creating modern, safe, and sustainable urban environments. International aid and donations played a significant role in these efforts, with contributions coming from various countries, organizations, and individuals who were moved by the plight of the survivors.

One of the critical challenges in rebuilding Nagasaki was addressing the environmental contamination caused by the atomic bomb. The radiation had rendered large areas of the city uninhabitable, and decontaminating the soil and water was a priority. Scientists and engineers worked tirelessly to clean up the affected areas, using innovative techniques to remove radioactive materials and restore the land to a safe condition.

As the physical reconstruction progressed, so did efforts to heal the social and psychological wounds inflicted by the bombing. The hibakusha, or atomic bomb survivors, faced not only the trauma of their experiences but also social stigma and discrimination. Many hibakusha suffered from severe burns, radiation sickness, and other long-term health effects. They also encountered prejudice and fear from others who believed, incorrectly, that radiation sickness was contagious or hereditary.

To support the hibakusha, various medical and psychological services were established. The Nagasaki Atomic Bomb Hospital, founded in the early post-war years, became a critical facility for treating the physical and mental health issues of the survivors. The government also provided financial assistance and social support programs to help the hibakusha rebuild their lives and integrate back into society.

The reconstruction of Nagasaki was not just about rebuilding structures but also about preserving memories and educating future generations. The Nagasaki Peace Park, established near the hypocenter of the blast, became a focal point for reflection and commemoration. The park features the iconic Peace Statue, a powerful symbol of hope and a reminder of the city's tragic past. The Nagasaki Atomic Bomb Museum, opened in 1955, offers a comprehensive account of the bombing, its aftermath, and the ongoing efforts towards nuclear disarmament.

Education played a pivotal role in Nagasaki's recovery. Schools and universities incorporated lessons about the atomic bombing into their curricula, ensuring that young people understood the significance of the events and the importance of peace. Peace education programs, workshops, and international exchange initiatives were developed to foster a culture of non-violence and global citizenship.

The economic recovery of Nagasaki was equally important. The city's industries, which had been a significant part of its identity and economy, were rebuilt and modernized. The Mitsubishi shipyards, steelworks, and other factories resumed operations, providing jobs and revitalising the local economy. Efforts were made to diversify the economy, attracting new businesses and fostering innovation in technology and other sectors.

Community rebuilding efforts were also crucial in reestablishing a sense of normalcy and resilience. Neighbourhoods were reconstructed with improved infrastructure and modern amenities. Cultural and social institutions, such as theaters, libraries, and sports facilities, were rebuilt, offering spaces for community gatherings and activities. These efforts helped restore the social fabric of the city, providing residents with opportunities to reconnect and support one another.

Nagasaki's journey of reconstruction was not just a story of physical rebuilding but also one of spiritual and emotional healing. The hibakusha, despite their suffering, emerged as powerful advocates for peace and nuclear disarmament. They shared their stories with the world, becoming voices for those who could no longer speak. Their testimonies were instrumental in raising global awareness about the horrors of nuclear warfare and the urgent need for disarmament.

One of the most remarkable aspects of Nagasaki's recovery was the city's commitment to reconciliation and international friendship. Recognizing the importance of building bridges with other nations, Nagasaki established sister city relationships with cities around the world, fostering cultural exchange and mutual understanding. These relationships helped promote a message of peace and solidarity, reinforcing the city's role as a global advocate for non-violence.

As the years passed, Nagasaki continued to evolve and grow. The city's rebuilt skyline, with its modern buildings and bustling streets, stands in stark contrast to the ruins of the past. Yet, amidst this progress, the memory of the atomic bombing remains a central part of Nagasaki's identity. Annual memorial ceremonies, held on August 9, serve as a solemn reminder of the city's history and a call to action for a peaceful future.

The story of Nagasaki's reconstruction is a testament to the resilience and determination of its people. From the ashes of destruction, they rebuilt their city and their lives, creating a vibrant and dynamic community committed to peace and justice. The lessons of Nagasaki continue to inspire people around the world, reminding us of the enduring human spirit and the power of collective action in the face of adversity.

Nagasaki's journey from devastation to recovery is a powerful narrative of hope and renewal. It underscores the importance of memory and education in preventing future tragedies, and it highlights the need for ongoing efforts towards nuclear disarmament and global peace. As we reflect on Nagasaki's legacy, we are reminded of our shared responsibility to build a world where such horrors are never repeated, and where the values of compassion, resilience, and peace prevail.

# CHAPTER TWENTY-TWO

# Global Reactions and Implications: The Aftermath of Nagasaki

The atomic bombing of Nagasaki on August 9, 1945, was met with a complex mix of reactions from around the world. The event not only marked a pivotal moment in World War II but also ushered in a new era in global geopolitics and ethical considerations regarding the use of nuclear weapons.

American Media and Public Reaction

In the United States, the initial reports on the bombing of Nagasaki were largely triumphant. Major newspapers like The New York Times and The Washington Post highlighted the strategic success of the bombing in hastening Japan's surrender and potentially saving countless lives that would have been lost in a prolonged war. President Harry S. Truman justified the use of the bomb as a necessary measure to end the war swiftly and to avoid further American casualties.

British Reaction

In the United Kingdom, the response was somewhat similar, with media outlets like The Times praising the decision to use the bomb to bring a swift end to the conflict. However, there was also a significant ethical debate among British intellectuals and political leaders. Winston Churchill expressed support for the action, emphasizing the bomb's role in saving lives by preventing a prolonged war. Nonetheless, there was growing concern about the implications of nuclear weapons and their future use in warfare.

Soviet Union's Perspective

The Soviet Union had a different perspective, marked by a mix of public solidarity with the Allies and private concern over the balance of power. Premier Joseph Stalin recognized the strategic advantage that the United States had gained and accelerated the Soviet nuclear program in response. Soviet newspapers, under tight state control, echoed the necessity of the bombings but emphasized the need for the Soviet Union to develop its own nuclear capabilities to counterbalance American power.

Japanese Reaction

In Japan, the bombings of Hiroshima and Nagasaki were met with profound horror and disbelief. The destruction was beyond anything the Japanese had experienced, leading to Emperor Hirohito's decision to surrender. The Japanese media, heavily censored and controlled by the wartime government, initially downplayed the severity of the bombings. However, as the extent of the devastation became undeniable, there was a shift towards accepting the Allied terms of surrender to prevent further suffering.

Global Ethical and Moral Debate

Around the world, the bombings prompted a vigorous ethical debate. Religious leaders, including Pope Pius XII, condemned the bombings, calling for a return to Christian values and the pursuit of peace through non-violent means. Intellectuals and philosophers questioned the morality of using such a weapon, arguing that the indiscriminate killing of civilians could not be justified by military necessity.

International Diplomacy and Peace Movements

The bombings had significant implications for international diplomacy. They highlighted the urgent need for mechanisms to control the spread of nuclear weapons. This led to the establishment of the United Nations and subsequent treaties aimed at preventing nuclear proliferation. The horror of the bombings galvanized the global peace movement, with activists like Albert Einstein and Bertrand Russell advocating for nuclear disarmament.

Cultural and Historical Legacy

The legacy of the Nagasaki bombing is also deeply embedded in global culture and history. The hibakusha, or atomic bomb survivors, became powerful advocates for peace, sharing their stories to educate the world about the horrors of nuclear warfare. Their testimonies have been crucial in fostering a global consciousness about the need for nuclear disarmament and the ethical responsibilities of those who possess such weapons.

In summary, the bombing of Nagasaki had a profound impact on global politics, ethical debates, and the collective consciousness of the world. It marked the beginning of the nuclear age and set the stage for ongoing efforts to prevent the proliferation of nuclear weapons and to promote global peace. The varied reactions from different countries underscore the complexity of this pivotal moment in history.

# Epilouge

## World Media Coverage of successive Nuclear Explosion

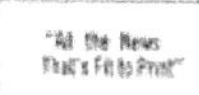

**The New York Times.**



### SOVIET DECLARES WAR ON JAPAN; ATTACKS MANCHURIA, TOKYO SAYS; ATOM BOMB LOOSED ON NAGASAKI

Report carried in the New York Times

**Fictionalized Discussion of the Potsdam Conference**

Context: Discussion on the Future of Germany and Eastern Europe

Date: July 20, 1945

Location: Cecilienhof Palace, Potsdam, Germany

Participants:

President Harry S. Truman (United States)

Premier Joseph Stalin (Soviet Union)

Prime Minister Winston Churchill (United Kingdom) (later replaced by Clement Attlee)

Foreign Minister Vyacheslav Molotov (Soviet Union)

Secretary of State James Byrnes (United States)

Foreign Secretary Anthony Eden (United Kingdom)

President Harry S. Truman: Gentlemen, we have convened here to determine the future of Germany and ensure that it never again poses a threat to world peace. We must agree on the principles of demilitarisation, denazification, and democratisation.

Premier Joseph Stalin: Agreed, Mr. President. The Soviet Union has suffered greatly from the German aggression. It is imperative that Germany is disarmed and that fascist elements are eradicated. We must also ensure that the reparations compensate for the destruction caused.

Prime Minister Winston Churchill: Indeed. The British Empire also demands justice. However, we must balance retribution with the need for a stable Europe. Excessive reparations could destabilise Germany and lead to future conflicts. We should focus on rebuilding Europe, including Germany, to prevent the rise of extremism.

Secretary of State James Byrnes: The United States proposes that Germany be divided into occupation zones, each controlled by the Allied powers. Berlin, though within the Soviet zone, should be similarly divided to ensure a balanced administration.

Foreign Minister Vyacheslav Molotov: We agree to the division, but the Soviet Union must receive adequate reparations. We propose that reparations be taken from each zone, with additional resources from the Western zones transferred to the Soviet Union.

Foreign Secretary Anthony Eden: This arrangement can be workable, but we must ensure that the reparations do not cripple Germany's economy entirely. A sustainable and balanced approach is essential for long-term peace.

Context: Discussion on the War in the Pacific and Japan's Surrender

President Harry S. Truman: Moving on to the war in the Pacific, we need to finalize our strategy to bring Japan to unconditional surrender. The Potsdam Declaration should clearly outline the terms and the consequences if Japan refuses.

Premier Joseph Stalin: The Soviet Union is prepared to enter the war against Japan, as agreed at Yalta. This will increase the pressure on Japan to surrender. However, we must ensure coordination of our military efforts.

Prime Minister Winston Churchill: The declaration must be firm but offer a clear path for Japan to surrender honourably. The use of overwhelming force, including strategic bombing and naval blockades, will be crucial.

Secretary of State James Byrnes: The United States is ready to issue the Potsdam Declaration. It should make clear that failure to surrender will result in prompt and utter destruction. We have a new weapon that could expedite Japan's decision.

Premier Joseph Stalin: A new weapon? What do you mean, Mr. Byrnes?

President Harry S. Truman: We have successfully tested an atomic bomb. This weapon has the potential to end the war swiftly. We must consider its use to avoid a prolonged and costly invasion of Japan.

Prime Minister Winston Churchill: This is indeed a significant development. The use of such a weapon could save countless lives, both Allied and Japanese. We must, however, carefully consider the implications of its use.

Foreign Minister Vyacheslav Molotov: If this weapon can end the war quickly, it should be used. The Soviet Union supports any measure that will bring about Japan's unconditional surrender.

Context: Discussion on Eastern Europe and Soviet Influence

President Harry S. Truman: We must also address the political situation in Eastern Europe. Free elections and democratic governance are essential for these liberated nations. The principles of the Atlantic Charter must be upheld.

Premier Joseph Stalin: The Soviet Union has legitimate security concerns in Eastern Europe. The governments in these countries must be friendly to the Soviet Union to prevent future threats. We will ensure that democratic processes are respected, but the composition of governments must guarantee Soviet security.

Prime Minister Winston Churchill: While we understand Soviet security concerns, we must insist on genuinely free and fair elections. The people of Eastern Europe should have the right to choose their own governments without outside interference.

Foreign Secretary Anthony Eden: The establishment of democratic institutions is critical for lasting peace. We propose the establishment of international commissions to oversee elections and ensure their fairness.

Premier Joseph Stalin: The Soviet Union will not accept interference in its sphere of influence. We have liberated these nations and will ensure that their governments are stable and friendly. The imposition of Western-style democracy is not suitable for all countries.

Secretary of State James Byrnes: We must find a compromise that respects both Soviet security concerns and the principles of self-determination. The future of Europe depends on our ability to cooperate and maintain stability.

Conclusion of the Meeting

President Harry S. Truman: We have made significant progress today. While there are differences, we must continue to work together to ensure a just and lasting peace. The decisions we make here will shape the future of the world.

Premier Joseph Stalin: The Soviet Union is committed to cooperation with our Allies. We must ensure that the sacrifices of our people during the war lead to a stable and secure future.

Prime Minister Winston Churchill: Agreed. Let us strive to create a world where such conflicts never happen again. We owe it to future generations to build a lasting peace.

Foreign Minister Vyacheslav Molotov: The details will be challenging, but with mutual respect and understanding, we can achieve our goals.

Secretary of State James Byrnes: Let us continue to negotiate in good faith and with the shared vision of a peaceful and prosperous world.

This fictionalised account provides a plausible representation of the key issues and discussions that took place at the Potsdam Conference. The actual conversations would have been more complex and nuanced, but this dialogue captures the essence of the negotiations and the differing perspectives of the Allied leaders.

**Fictionalized Discussion of the Versailles Meeting**

Context: Discussion on the Racial Equality Proposal and Japan's Role

Date: April 11, 1919

Location: Versailles, France

Participants:

Prime Minister Hara Takashi (Japan)

Baron Makino Nobuaki (Japan)

President Woodrow Wilson (United States)

Prime Minister David Lloyd George (United Kingdom)

Prime Minister Georges Clemenceau (France)

Prime Minister Hara Takashi: Gentlemen, thank you for convening. Japan wishes to propose an amendment to the Covenant of the League of Nations. We seek the inclusion of a clause that promotes racial equality among all member nations. We believe that recognizing racial equality is essential for fostering genuine international cooperation and peace.

President Woodrow Wilson: Prime Minister Hara, we understand the importance of your proposal. However, the League's primary focus should be on establishing mechanisms for preventing future conflicts and ensuring collective security.

Prime Minister David Lloyd George: While we appreciate Japan's contributions during the war, the racial equality clause might create significant domestic challenges. For instance, in the British Empire, we have a diverse array of cultures and races, and such a clause could complicate our colonial administration.

Baron Makino Nobuaki: Our proposal aims to affirm the principle that all nations and peoples are equal, deserving of respect and fair treatment. This is not only a matter of principle but also one of justice and international solidarity.

Prime Minister Georges Clemenceau: France understands Japan's position, especially considering your significant role in the war. However, we must consider the political realities and the potential backlash in our colonies and among our electorate.

Prime Minister Hara Takashi: The rejection of this proposal could be seen as a denial of Japan's equal status among the Great Powers. It may foster resentment and undermine the spirit of cooperation we are trying to build.

President Woodrow Wilson: We must proceed with caution. The inclusion of such a clause may alienate many nations who are currently wary of the League's broader objectives. We must ensure the League's foundation is stable and acceptable to all.

Baron Makino Nobuaki: If the League is to promote lasting peace, it must do so on the basis of equality and mutual respect. By rejecting this proposal, we risk perpetuating the very inequalities that lead to conflict.

Prime Minister David Lloyd George: We propose that we defer the discussion on racial equality to a later date. The immediate task at hand is to secure the League's establishment and address the pressing issues of reparations and territorial adjustments.

Prime Minister Hara Takashi: This is disappointing, but we will defer to the consensus for now. However, I must stress that Japan's cooperation hinges on being treated with the respect and equality that we afford to all other nations.

**Context: Discussion on Reparations and Territorial Adjustments**

President Woodrow Wilson: Moving on to the matter of reparations. It is imperative that Germany compensates for the immense damage caused during the war. However, we must ensure that the reparations are fair and do not cripple Germany's economy to the point where it fosters future resentment and conflict.

Prime Minister Georges Clemenceau: France has borne the brunt of the devastation. Our people demand justice and reparations that reflect the severity of our suffering. We must hold Germany accountable.

Prime Minister David Lloyd George: We agree that Germany must pay for the damage, but we must also consider the economic stability of Europe. Excessive reparations could lead to economic collapse, which is in no one's interest.

Prime Minister Hara Takashi: Japan supports reasonable reparations that ensure justice while maintaining economic stability. Additionally, we seek recognition of our territorial gains in the Pacific and China, which are essential for our security and economic interests.

President Woodrow Wilson: Regarding territorial adjustments, it is crucial that we respect the principle of self-determination. The territories in question should have the opportunity to determine their own future.

Prime Minister Georges Clemenceau: Self-determination is a noble principle, but practical considerations must prevail. We cannot ignore the strategic and economic needs of the victorious powers.

Prime Minister David Lloyd George: The balance between self-determination and strategic interests is delicate. We must strive for solutions that ensure long-term stability and peace.

Baron Makino Nobuaki: Japan insists on the recognition of its control over the former German territories in the Pacific and

Shandong. This recognition is vital for our national security and economic interests.

President Woodrow Wilson: We will acknowledge Japan's contributions and territorial claims, but we must ensure that these claims do not undermine the broader principles we are establishing for a stable post-war order.

Prime Minister Hara Takashi: Japan's interests are aligned with the goal of lasting peace and stability. We seek fair treatment and recognition of our status as a major power.

Conclusion of the Meeting

President Woodrow Wilson: We have covered significant ground today. While there are differences, I believe we can reach agreements that balance justice, fairness, and stability. The decisions we make here will shape the future of international relations and peace.

Prime Minister Georges Clemenceau: Let us ensure that the sacrifices made during the war are honoured through our commitment to a just and lasting peace.

Prime Minister David Lloyd George: Agreed. We must build a world where future generations are spared the horrors we have witnessed.

Prime Minister Hara Takashi: Japan remains committed to the principles of peace and cooperation. We trust that our contributions and concerns will be given the respect they deserve.

Baron Makino Nobuaki: Let us work together to create a framework that ensures stability, justice, and mutual respect among all nations.

Historical Context and Verbatim Discussion

Historical Context

During the Potsdam Conference, held from July 17 to August 2, 1945, President Truman received confirmation of the successful test of the atomic bomb, known as the Trinity Test, on July 16, 1945. This information significantly influenced the discussions about Japan and the strategy to bring about its surrender.

**Discussion Based on Historical Records**

The exact conversation was not transcribed verbatim, but historical records provide insights into the exchange between Truman and Stalin regarding the atomic bomb. Here is a reconstructed account based on documented interactions:

Date: July 24, 1945

Location: Cecilienhof Palace, Potsdam, Germany

Participants:

President Harry S. Truman (United States)

Premier Joseph Stalin (Soviet Union)

Secretary of State James Byrnes (United States)

President Harry S. Truman: Premier Stalin, I wanted to inform you that the United States now possesses a new weapon of unusual destructive force. We have successfully developed a powerful new bomb, which we believe can bring the war with Japan to a swift end.

Premier Joseph Stalin: I see. I hope you will make good use of this new weapon against the Japanese.

President Harry S. Truman: We are considering all our options to bring about a quick and decisive end to the conflict.

Premier Joseph Stalin: That is good. We will join the war against Japan as agreed at Yalta.

President Harry S. Truman: We appreciate your commitment. Together, we will ensure that Japan surrenders unconditionally and that peace is restored.

Analysis

Truman's Disclosure: Truman's mention of a "new weapon of unusual destructive force" was deliberately vague. He did not provide specific details about the atomic bomb, its capabilities, or the fact that it had been successfully tested.

Stalin's Reaction: Stalin's reaction was notably understated. Historical accounts suggest that Stalin already had some knowledge about the American atomic bomb project through Soviet intelligence. However, his response in the meeting was deliberately measured, possibly to avoid revealing this knowledge.

Strategic Implications: The disclosure was significant because it highlighted the new power dynamic emerging from the development of nuclear weapons. It also set the stage for the atomic bombings of Hiroshima and Nagasaki in August 1945, which ultimately led to Japan's surrender.

While President Truman did inform Premier Stalin about the existence of a new and powerful weapon during the Potsdam Conference, the conversation was brief and lacked specific details about the atomic bomb. This carefully controlled disclosure was part of the broader strategic considerations that influenced the end of World War II and the early stages of the Cold War.

The decision to use the atomic bomb was primarily made by U.S. officials, including President Harry S. Truman and his top advisors, rather than during an international meeting. However, there were discussions at the Potsdam Conference regarding the use of the bomb and the strategy for ending the war with Japan. Here is a reconstructed, fictionalized verbatim account of such a discussion based on historical context:

**Discussion on the Decision to Drop the Atomic Bomb**

Date: July 24, 1945

Location: Cecilienhof Palace, Potsdam, Germany

Participants:

President Harry S. Truman (United States)

Secretary of State James Byrnes (United States)

General George Marshall (United States)

General Leslie Groves (United States)

Premier Joseph Stalin (Soviet Union) (briefly informed)

Prime Minister Winston Churchill (United Kingdom) (before being replaced by Clement Attlee)

President Harry S. Truman: Gentlemen, we have received confirmation of the successful test of the atomic bomb. This weapon has unprecedented destructive power. We need to discuss its potential use to bring about Japan's unconditional surrender.

Secretary of State James Byrnes: Mr. President, the use of this bomb could save countless American and Allied lives by avoiding a prolonged invasion of Japan. The Japanese have shown no indication of surrendering despite the extensive bombing campaigns and the blockade.

General George Marshall: The invasion of Japan, scheduled to begin in November, is expected to result in significant casualties on both sides. The bomb could compel Japan to surrender without the need for an invasion, which would save many lives.

General Leslie Groves: The test in New Mexico demonstrated the bomb's immense power. Its use would send a clear message of our capabilities and might prevent future conflicts by establishing a strong deterrent.

President Harry S. Truman: Prime Minister Churchill, what are your thoughts on this matter?

Prime Minister Winston Churchill: The bomb's potential to end the war swiftly is compelling. We must also consider the geopolitical implications. Demonstrating such power will undoubtedly influence post-war negotiations and our standing against the Soviets.

Secretary of State James Byrnes: We should also consider issuing a final ultimatum to Japan, warning them of the consequences if they do not surrender. The Potsdam Declaration can serve this purpose, but we must be prepared to act if they refuse.

President Harry S. Truman: Agreed. We will issue the Potsdam Declaration, warning Japan of "prompt and utter destruction" if they do not surrender. If they fail to comply, we will proceed with the use of the atomic bomb.

General George Marshall: We should select targets that have significant military value but also demonstrate the bomb's destructive power. Hiroshima and Nagasaki are viable options.

Prime Minister Winston Churchill: The decision is a grave one, but the potential to end the war and save lives makes it a necessary consideration. Let us proceed with caution and resolve.

President Harry S. Truman: Very well. We will proceed with the issuance of the Potsdam Declaration and prepare for the potential use of the atomic bomb if Japan does not surrender. General Marshall, General Groves, you will oversee the preparations.

**Brief Informing of Premier Joseph Stalin**

President Harry S. Truman: Premier Stalin, I wanted to inform you that the United States now possesses a new weapon of unusual destructive force. We have successfully developed a powerful new bomb, which we believe can bring the war with Japan to a swift end.

Premier Joseph Stalin: I see. I hope you will make good use of this new weapon against the Japanese.

President Harry S. Truman: We are considering all our options to bring about a quick and decisive end to the conflict.

Premier Joseph Stalin: That is good. We will join the war against Japan as agreed at Yalta.

President Harry S. Truman: We appreciate your commitment. Together, we will ensure that Japan surrenders unconditionally and that peace is restored.

This fictionalized account provides a plausible representation of the key discussions that would have taken place regarding the decision to use the atomic bomb. The actual conversations were more complex and involved additional considerations, but this dialogue captures the essence of the strategic, ethical, and geopolitical deliberations that influenced the decision.

**Discussion between President Truman and J. Robert Oppenheimer**

Date: July 25, 1945

Location: White House, Washington, D.C. (prior to Truman's departure to Potsdam)

Participants:

President Harry S. Truman (United States)

J. Robert Oppenheimer (Scientific Director of the Manhattan Project)

Secretary of War Henry Stimson (United States)

General Leslie Groves (United States)

President Harry S. Truman: Dr. Oppenheimer, thank you for coming. I've been briefed on the success of the Trinity test. This is indeed a monumental achievement. I'd like to hear your perspective on the bomb and its potential use against Japan.

J. Robert Oppenheimer: Mr. President, the test was successful beyond our expectations. The device detonated with a force equivalent to 20,000 tons of TNT. The scientific and technical teams have worked tirelessly, and we now have a weapon of unprecedented destructive power.

President Harry S. Truman: How confident are you in the bomb's reliability and its ability to bring about Japan's surrender?

J. Robert Oppenheimer: The bomb is reliable, and its destructive capability is immense. If used on a major city, it could cause unprecedented damage and loss of life, potentially compelling Japan to surrender. However, I must express a concern. The ethical implications of using such a weapon are profound. The immediate impact will be catastrophic for any target city and its inhabitants.

Secretary of War Henry Stimson: Dr. Oppenheimer, we understand the gravity of the decision. The primary goal is to end the war swiftly and save lives, both American and Japanese. The Japanese military has shown a willingness to fight to the last man. We believe this demonstration of power will force them to reconsider.

General Leslie Groves: Mr. President, the military value of this weapon is clear. It will send a strong message not only to Japan but also to the world. We must also consider the post-war implications and the signal it sends about American strength and technological capability.

President Harry S. Truman: Dr. Oppenheimer, do you believe there is any alternative to using the bomb that would achieve the same result?

J. Robert Oppenheimer: Mr. President, alternatives such as a demonstration or continued conventional bombing might not have the same immediate impact on the Japanese leadership. The psychological shock of an actual attack on a city could be decisive. However, I urge caution and reflection on the long-term consequences of introducing nuclear weapons into warfare.

President Harry S. Truman: This is a difficult decision, but our primary responsibility is to end the war and save lives. We will proceed with issuing the Potsdam Declaration, warning Japan of the consequences if they do not surrender. If they refuse, we will use the bomb. Dr. Oppenheimer, thank you for your contributions and for sharing your concerns. Your work has brought us to a critical juncture in history.

J. Robert Oppenheimer: Thank you, Mr. President. I understand the gravity of your decision and trust that it will be made with the utmost consideration for humanity's future.

President Harry S. Truman: It will be. General Groves, proceed with the preparations. Secretary Stimson, let's finalize the wording of the Potsdam Declaration.

This fictionalized account represents a plausible reconstruction of the type of conversation that might have occurred between President Truman and J. Robert Oppenheimer. The actual conversations were private and not fully documented, but the key themes and considerations are consistent with historical records and the known positions of the participants.